D0913895

NORTH AMERICAN
RAILROAD FAMILY TREES

An Infographic History of the Industry's Mergers and Evolution

BRIAN SOLOMON

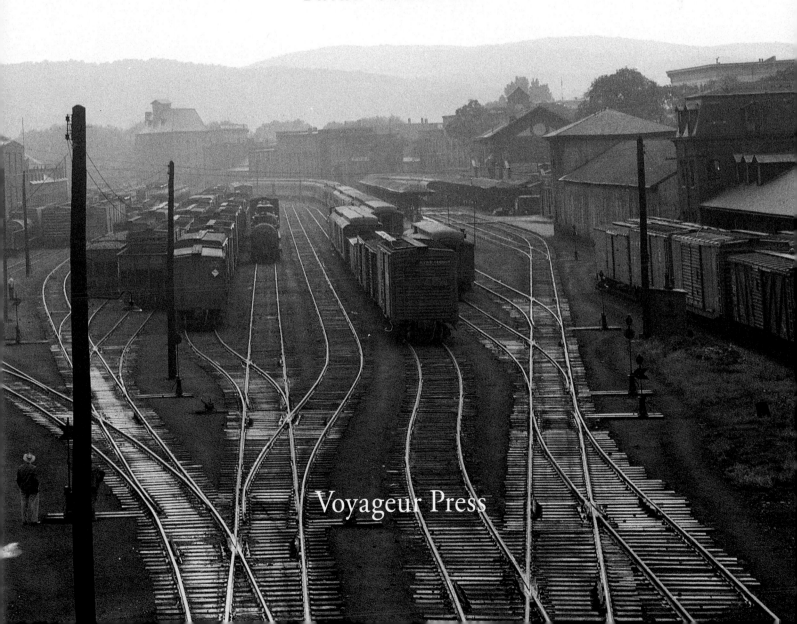

Voyageur Press

First published in 2013 by Voyageur Press, an imprint of MBI Publishing Company,
400 First Avenue North, Suite 400, Minneapolis, MN 55401 USA

Voyageur Press titles are also available at discounts in bulk quantity for industrial or sales-promotional use.
For details write to Special Sales Manager at MBI Publishing Company, 400 First Avenue North, Suite 400,
Minneapolis, MN 55401 USA.

To find out more about our books, visit us online at www.voyageurpress.com.

Library of Congress Cataloging-in-Publication Data

Solomon, Brian, 1966-
   North American railroad family trees : an infographic history of the industry's mergers and evolution / Brian Solomon.
      p. cm.
   Includes bibliographical references and index.
   ISBN 978-0-7603-4488-0 (hc)
   1. Railroads--North America--History. 2. Railroads--Mergers--North America--History. 3. Railroad companies--North
America--History. I. Title.
   HE2751.S65 2013
   385.0973--dc23
                              2013014156

Commissioning Editor: Dennis Pernu
Design Manager: Cindy Samargia Laun
Designer: Simon Larkin
Design and Layout: Chris Fayers
Illustrator: Mandy Kimlinger

Frontis: A mechanic changes a headlight on an Illinois Central 9600 at Clinton, Illinois, on June 9, 1989. This locomotive
carried the name of IC's most famous engineer, Casey Jones, killed in a train wreck in 1900. *Scott Muskopf*

Title page: Rutland, Vermont, was the heart of the Rutland Railroad system where the railroad had shops and yards (pictured).
Early in the twentieth century, Rutland was among lines in the Vanderbilt sphere. It connected with the Boston & Albany via its
"Corkscrew Division" at Chatham, New York, and with other New York Central system lines at junctions in upstate New York.
John E. Pickett

Printed in China

CONTENTS

ACKNOWLEDGMENTS

My interest in railroad family trees goes back to my teenage years in the early 1980s, when I used to delve into my father's timetable collection to pore over the maps and schedules of railroads long departed. I wondered what had happened to the many colorful railroads of yesteryear: the Northern Pacific, Lehigh Valley, Nickel Plate Road, and Texas & Pacific. What was the Spokane, Portland & Seattle? Later, as I learned a bit of merger history, I'd draw diagrams similar to those inside this book. But the real story behind the reasons why the railroads had merged still eluded me. At that time, the railroad merger movement was regaining momentum after a period of relative quiet. I made a project of writing to each major American railroad asking for information. All responded, even the Frisco, which had just been absorbed by Burlington Northern. In the process, I added to my father's timetable collection with schedules from Amtrak, VIA Rail, and the various commuter lines.

As my interest matured, I began to understand the details of American railroad history. My late friend, Bob Buck of Tucker's Hobbies, generously loaned me railroad literature—books by S. Kip Farrington, Alvin Fay Harlow, and others. I scoured my father's library, reading histories of the New York, Ontario & Western, Nickel Plate Road, and everything on the Pennsylvania Railroad and New York Central systems, plus all of William D. Middleton's excellent books. Years later, as my interests broadened, I discovered books by John F. Stover, Edward Hungerford, John Signor, and others while leafing through back issues of *Trains* and *Railway Age*. Conrail planning documents found their way into my dad's collection, and among these obscure publications was *Rail Service in the Midwest and Northeast Region*, prepared by the secretary of transportation.

Another revelation was Richard Saunders's original work, *Railroad Mergers and the Coming of Conrail*, which was the first book that really helped me understand the changes to mid-twentieth-century railroading. In more recent times, I've read his follow-up books on railroad mergers while researching my own books on Conrail, Amtrak, CSX, and other topics.

In the mid-1990s, when I edited *Pacific RailNews* at Pentrex Publishing and assisted with other titles, it seemed as if the entire industry was alive with merger: Burlington Northern plus Santa Fe; Wisconsin Central plus Algoma Central; Union Pacific plus Chicago & North Western and Southern Pacific, in addition to various other proposed combinations. I had numerous discussions with my columnists, authors, and industry professionals about the state of the industry and its future. Mike Blaszak was especially helpful, offering great insights into regulatory issues and other driving forces, while Mark Hemphill raised thought-provoking questions regarding the UP-SP merger.

In the lead-up to this project, I consulted more than 150 published sources, the most relevant of which are listed in the bibliography. In addition, over the years, I've conducted candid conversations with numerous friends in the industry. The Irish Railway Record Society allowed me unlimited access to their library in Dublin, and I've conducted research at the UMass Amherst Libraries, the Wendt Library at the University of Wisconsin in Madison, San Francisco's Public Library at the San Francisco Civic Center, Steamtown's archives in Scranton, Pennsylvania, and the Railroad Museum of Pennsylvania at Strasburg. In addition, I've borrowed materials from many friends, including Bob Buck, Kenneth Buck, Sylvia Buck, Tim Doherty, Doug Eisele, John Gruber, Chris Guss, Brian Jennison, Bill Keay, Fred Matthews, Doug Moore, Rich Reed, David Swirk, Otto Vondrak, and Patrick Yough.

Special thanks to all the photographers who loaned images for this project, each of whom is credited alongside their work. My father, Richard Jay Solomon, assisted with research and proofreading. My editor, Dennis Pernu, helped conceive the idea for this book and see it through to completion. Thanks to gifted artist Andy Fletcher for his faithful adaptations of traditional paint schemes on Norfolk Southern's thirtieth-anniversary heritage fleet. Also, thanks to my brother, Sean Solomon, who has accompanied me on trips over the years, as have many of those friends already mentioned. May you enjoy this book and find it enlightening!

Northern Pacific's Chicago-Seattle *North Coast Limited* was among America's finest streamliners. Despite losses, NP didn't allow deterioration of its passenger trains. Burlington Northern took over in March 1970, and here BN's *North Coast Limited* meets a freight led by a freshly painted BN GP9, shortly before Amtrak assumed operation of intercity passenger services on May 1, 1971. *Richard Jay Solomon*

7

INTRODUCTION

The present North American railway network has its origins in thousands of railroad companies that over the years have been melded together in various ways to form seven vast freight railways, hundreds of short-line and regional systems, and a host of publicly funded passenger networks. As railroads have come together, new corporate banners have replaced classic railroad names. For example, today's CSXT represents routes formerly operated by more than a dozen classic late-steam-era railroads, including companies as varied as the old Monon, Western Maryland, and Richmond, Fredericksburg & Potomac.

While the large railroads have swallowed up most of the old lines, a few classic names survive. Florida East Coast has served essentially the same route since the end of steam. Though FEC is owned by a major corporation, it hasn't been blended into one of the massive railroad networks. The name Union Pacific is one of the oldest in the industry. As one of the two dominant freight railroads in the West, UP is far more today than the name applied to its historic route structure. UP now consists of the old Missouri Pacific, Southern Pacific, and Rio Grande systems, among other notable western lines. Other classic railroad names survive solely on paper or exist as latent components of larger systems.

A SUMMATION OF HISTORY

In the early twentieth century, while there were a great number of individual carriers, most were effectively controlled by just a handful of men. One analyst identified just 17 systems that represented the majority of railway mileage and traffic. The nature of the business at that time enabled individual railroad companies to retain both their identity and a high degree of independence even when controlled by another line. However, financial groupings alarmed many observers because, before effective competition from other modes, railroad companies

A fleeting glimpse of Chicago & North Western in May 1995, weeks before it was absorbed by Union Pacific. The sun sets as C&NW's former Rock Island GP7s switch at Jefferson Junction, Wisconsin. *Brian Solomon*

MORTON SALT

Empire State Express, going east from Schenectady, N. Y

To overcome a decade of bad publicity stemming from the cavalier attitude of its owners and several catastrophic accidents, New York Central carried out well-orchestrated advertising campaigns to glamorize its trains. Its famed *Empire State Express* is pictured east of Schenectady, New York, on this early-twentieth-century postcard. *Solomon collection*

controlled virtually all of American transportation. A public backlash resulted when it appeared that economic "trusts" were forming among the most important railroads. Federal legislation and subsequent judicial decisions broke up many of the early-twentieth-century railroad systems. While some, such as James J. Hill's railroads, retained family relationships, other systems were fragmented, with their component railroads set loose to form new ties.

The essential complexities of railroad families, combined with a host of opaque mechanisms of big business, make it difficult to simply describe how railroad systems emerged. In this book, the diagrams offer general clarifications. The first chapter deals with early railroad affiliations, illustrating the nature of dominant systems of the early twentieth century. The rest of the book focuses on combinations since World War I, specifically illustrating railroad mergers that either preceded or helped create the massive systems of today.

The family tree diagrams chart the incredibly complex railroad affiliations, including mergers, leases, holding companies, and new spinoff companies and public passenger agencies. However, among the perils of providing clearer visual interpretations comes the risk of oversimplification. By visually joining routes and companies, detailed explanations are obviated—the necessary negotiations among parties, changes to corporate structures, combining of union rosters, infrastructure revisions, altered traffic patterns, plus everything else that occurs as railroads are blended together or otherwise affiliated. The very nature of these diagrams incurs simplification, making it easier to see how the railroads came together.

Although Canada's major railroads are included in the family trees, this book largely focuses on Canadian railroad operations in the United States and not the details of recent changes specific to railroading in Canada. Likewise, Mexican lines are mentioned only where directly related to operations in the United States.

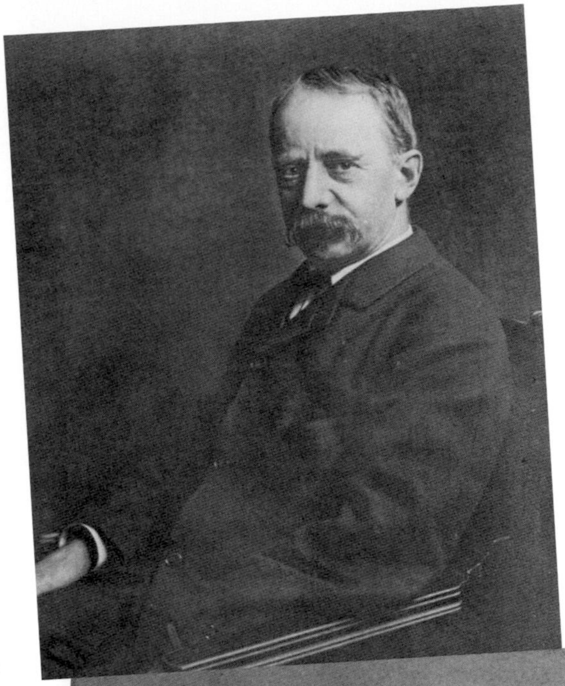

Edward Henry Harriman was one of the titans of western railroading. His efforts to consolidate Southern Pacific and Union Pacific led to one of the most complex court battles of railroading's Golden Age. *From a Harriman biography, Solomon collection*

VARIATIONS ON A THEME

Every railroad merger has been handled differently. Some have been executed relatively quickly, with the dominant railroad rapidly assimilating the acquired property, effectively erasing the identity of the merged line in just a few years. Other mergers have taken a more gradual approach, allowing component identities to survive for decades or generations despite control or total ownership by another company. Boston & Albany was part of the Vanderbilt sphere for more than a decade before New York Central & Hudson River formally leased it in 1900. In the first decade of the New York Central lease, Central's identity prevailed over B&A's, but public demands in Massachusetts encouraged Central to restore B&A's name to equipment, stations, and public literature, and maintain local management. This arrangement survived until the end of the steam era, when in the 1950s B&A quietly disappeared into the New York Central System.

In the modern era, the sheer size of some amalgamations have resulted in predecessors' equipment serving the new company in vintage paint for a decade or more, despite an old name having lost its relevance within the consolidated company. The 1996 merger of Union Pacific and Southern Pacific, for example, involved thousands of locomotives and tens of thousands of freight cars, so while there is no longer an operating entity known as SP, equipment survives in that railroad's paint scheme.

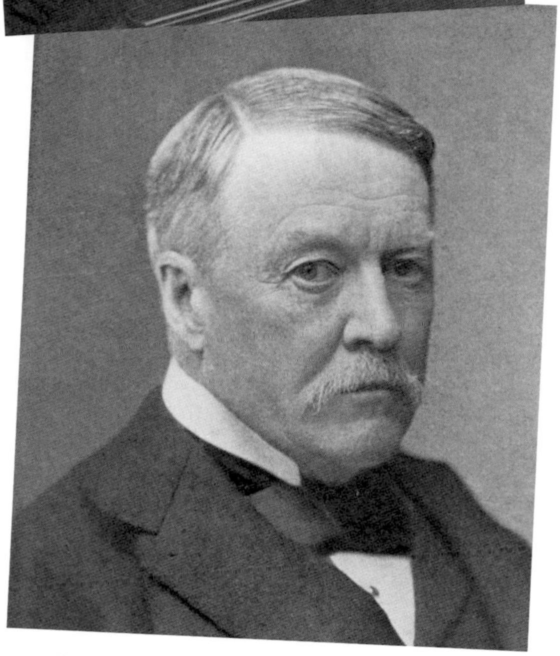

UNDERSTANDING THE DIAGRAMS

Industry observers, as well as railroaders, are always anticipating mergers, speculating about the results of past and present combinations and how they might affect the companies, people, locomotives, and traffic. Mergers don't necessarily mean that the sum of the merged railroads will be reflected in the combined track mileage or route structure of their components. In the decades of retrenchment, beginning in the 1950s, joining of parallel railroads typically resulted in downgraded mainlines, consolidation of yards and shops, and changes in traffic. Two decades after Chicago & North Western absorbed Minneapolis & St. Louis, virtually nothing remained of the latter railroad.

The intent of the charts is to display cleanly and accurately railroad mergers as reflected by their operations and the outward appearance of the companies involved. The proximity of lines in the diagrams demonstrates affiliations, while joined lines indicate the blending of one company with another. In some instances the corporate shell of a railroad survives after its railroad operations are merged into the enlarged company, but if it has little or no relevance in

In 1906, PRR was not only the greatest railroad in America, but it was also one of the world's leading companies. As Pennsylvania Railroad's most enlightened leader, Alexander Cassatt prepared the railroad for the twentieth century while enabling construction of infrastructure still crucial more than a century later. Had he not died prematurely, we might live in a different world today. *From a Pennsylvania Railroad company history, Solomon collection*

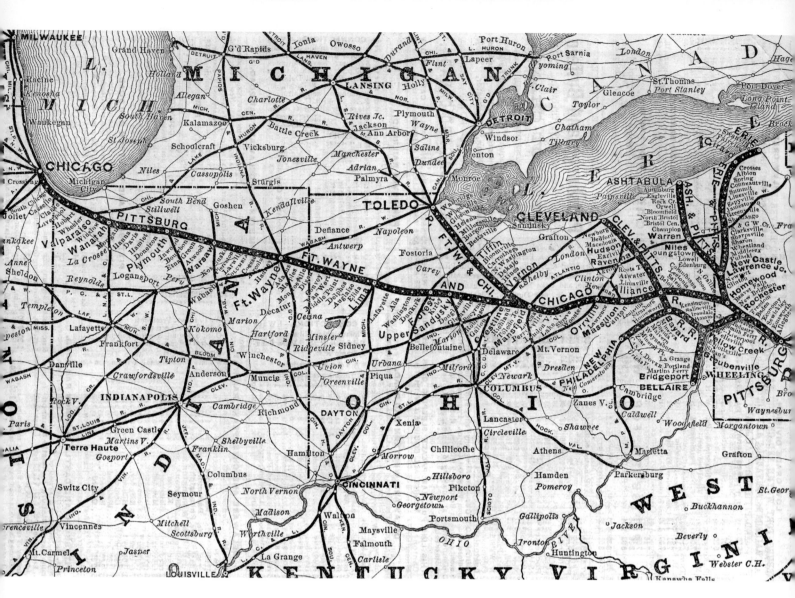

One of PRR's links to Chicago was the Pittsburg [sic], Fort Wayne & Chicago, as illustrated in this 1881 route map. *From August 1881 Travelers' Official Guide of Railroad and Steam Navigation Lines, Buck collection*

the day-to-day appearance of the new company, the corporate shell is shown as a joined line. Likewise, if companies that unified under a holding company or merger continue to function with a degree of independence, the lines are shown chronologically parallel and close until one company functionally ceases to exist. For example, diagrams that show Western Maryland reflect a complex pattern whereby WM was in Baltimore & Ohio's sphere of influence since the 1920s; by the 1960s it was effectively owned by the joint B&O/Chesapeake & Ohio system. While WM's lines were truncated during the 1970s, it survived as a railroad until it finally merged into B&O in 1982.

It is also important to realize that prior to formal affiliation many railroads have enjoyed reciprocal stock arrangements, common traffic, common officers, or other commonalities that may not necessarily be reflected in the diagrams and yet may have played a role in their history from birth to consolidation. To avoid indecipherable spaghetti bowls of lines while trying to accurately portray every notional affiliation, the diagrams opt for clarity, sometimes placing significant relationships in footnotes. Except for a few of the more detailed diagrams, crossing lines are avoided for simplicity.

How to Read a Railroad Family Tree

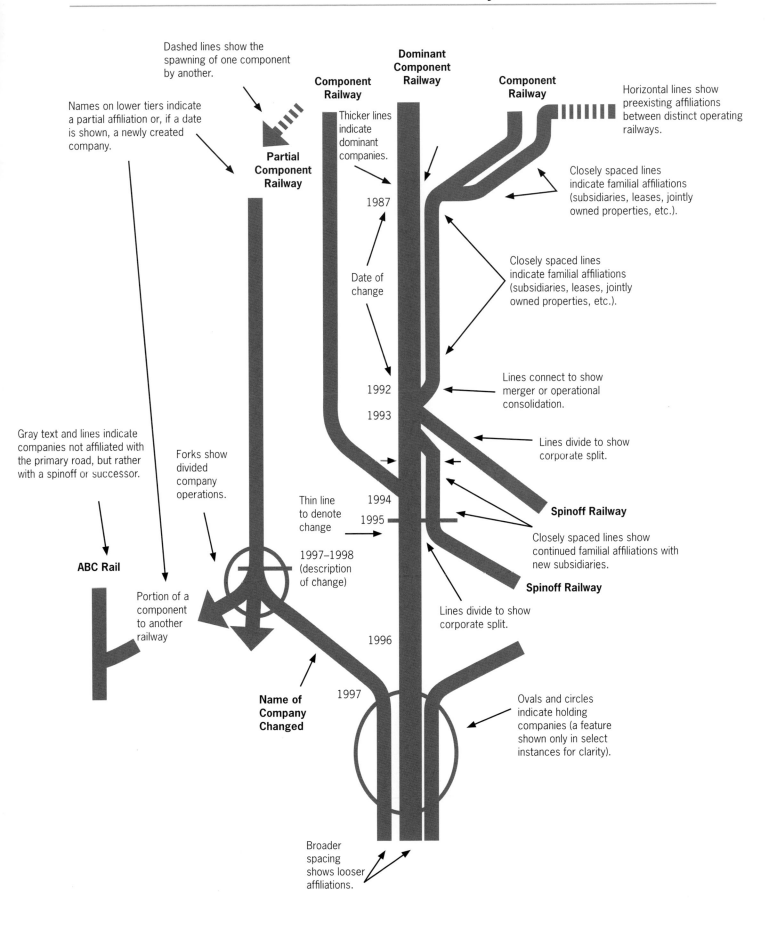

Dashed lines show the spawning of one component by another.

Names on lower tiers indicate a partial affiliation or, if a date is shown, a newly created company.

Component Railway

Dominant Component Railway

Component Railway

Horizontal lines show preexisting affiliations between distinct operating railways.

Thicker lines indicate dominant companies.

Partial Component Railway

1987

Date of change

Closely spaced lines indicate familial affiliations (subsidiaries, leases, jointly owned properties, etc.).

Closely spaced lines indicate familial affiliations (subsidiaries, leases, jointly owned properties, etc.).

1992

1993

Lines connect to show merger or operational consolidation.

Lines divide to show corporate split.

Gray text and lines indicate companies not affiliated with the primary road, but rather with a spinoff or successor.

Forks show divided company operations.

Thin line to denote change

1994

1995

Spinoff Railway

Closely spaced lines show continued familial affiliations with new subsidiaries.

ABC Rail

1997–1998 (description of change)

Spinoff Railway

Portion of a component to another railway

Lines divide to show corporate split.

Name of Company Changed

1996

1997

Ovals and circles indicate holding companies (a feature shown only in select instances for clarity).

Broader spacing shows looser affiliations.

Chapter 1

THE OLD FAMILIES

Affiliations of the Golden Age, 1900–1915

Southern Pacific 4-6-0 2248 leads a fire train on Donner Pass at Emigrant Gap, California. Fire trains were needed to protect the many miles of wooden snow sheds on Donner. SP's Central Pacific route and Union Pacific's mainlines were built together as America's first transcontinental route. These lines enjoyed unified management under E. H. Harriman, who invested heavily in infrastructure and safety improvements. However, the antitrust regime in Washington frowned on the combination, and following Harriman's death in 1909, lengthy court battles separated UP and SP, then unsuccessfully attempted to separate Central Pacific from SP. *John E. Pickett*

American railroads began as localized ventures. Many companies were locally owned and designed to connect nearby localities. The Boston & Lowell, New Haven & Hartford, and many others were aimed solely to serve their namesakes. While some projects envisioned larger scopes from their earliest days, they remained focused on specific regional objectives. The Baltimore & Ohio (1827) and the Western Railroad of Massachusetts (1833)—two of the most ambitious early railroads—were both designed to connect their respective port cities (Baltimore and Boston) with interior waterways. However, by the 1840s, railroads began to form affiliations and join together in ever-larger networks and systems. Railroads were melded in a variety of ways ranging from outright ownership, leveraged stock control, and leases to less formal affiliations through common officers and interlocking directorships. The range of these affiliations makes it difficult to decipher lines of control since in the nineteenth century some arrangements were deliberately convoluted.

In the 1850s, the string of railroads running from Albany to Buffalo joined forces as the original New York Central. By the 1860s, even more ambitious schemes were taking hold. Cornelius Vanderbilt, who had built a fortune in shipping, had shifted his focus to railroads in the 1850s, first taking control of the New York & Harlem and then expanding his hold to form the nucleus of an empire by merging the Harlem with the competing Hudson River Railroad and connecting the two with a new New York Central & Hudson River Railroad system. Meanwhile, the Pennsylvania Railroad was coalescing around a network with a hub in Philadelphia. Vanderbilt's system and PRR formed respective alliances with Midwestern lines to reach Chicago. For the next century, these two systems would vie to control traffic,

Cornelius Vanderbilt was founder of the New York Central System and the Vanderbilt dynasty. *The American Railway from 1893, Solomon collection*

Opposite: This 1889 map printed in *The American Railway* published in 1893 depicts the Pennsylvania Railroad and Vanderbilt networks on their ascent. It includes lines in their respective spheres of influence that were not yet in their total control. *The American Railway from 1893, Solomon collection*

territory, and prestige, while remaining the largest, most significant, and by far the most powerful railroads in North America. Cornelius died in 1877, but control of his transportation empire passed to key members of his family and the New York Central System and affiliated properties became part of the vast Vanderbilt empire.

As systems and networks developed, principal railroads connected at gateway cities to exchange traffic. The most important gateways were well-established at places where railroads met waterways—cities like Buffalo, Pittsburgh, Cincinnati, Louisville, Memphis, New Orleans, St. Louis, and the Twin Cities of Minneapolis-St. Paul. The biggest and most important gateway developed on the south shore of Lake Michigan at Chicago. Railroad companies built toward the Windy City from every region, and soon Chicago boasted more railroad terminuses than any other American city. The variety of lines reaching Chicago gave carriers the most interchange partners there and thus Chicago emerged as the primary east-west gateway. So, while many railroads reached Chicago, there was little incentive to reach beyond

The Vanderbilt system was centered on the New York Central & Hudson River Railroad; this early 1890s view depicts NYC&HRR's freight yards on the Manhattan waterfront. *The American Railway from 1893, Solomon collection*

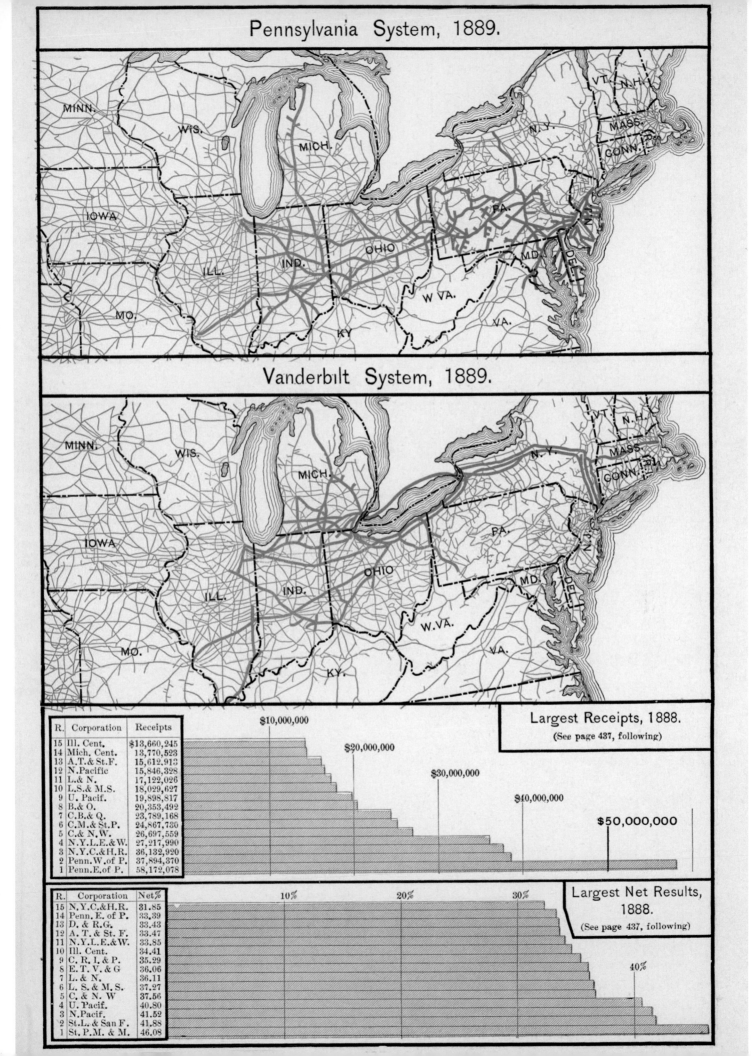

Pennsylvania System, 1889.

Vanderbilt System, 1889.

Largest Receipts, 1888.
(See page 437, following)

R.	Corporation	Receipts
15	Ill. Cent.	$13,660,245
14	Mich. Cent.	13,770,523
13	A.T.& St.F.	15,612,913
12	N.Pacific	15,846,328
11	L.& N.	17,122,026
10	L.S.& M.S.	18,029,627
9	U. Pacif.	19,898,817
8	B.& O.	20,353,492
7	C.B.& Q.	23,789,168
6	C.M.& St.P.	24,867,730
5	C.& N.W.	26,697,559
4	N.Y.L.E.&W.	27,217,990
3	N.Y.C.&H.R.	36,132,920
2	Penn.W.of P.	37,894,370
1	Penn.E.of P.	58,172,078

$10,000,000 $20,000,000 $30,000,000 $40,000,000 **$50,000,000**

Largest Net Results, 1888.
(See page 437, following)

R.	Corporation	Net%
15	N.Y.C.&H.R.	31.85
14	Penn. E. of P.	33.39
13	D. & R.G.	33.43
12	A. T. & St. F.	33.47
11	N.Y.L.E.&W.	33.85
10	Ill. Cent.	34.41
9	C. R. I. & P.	35.29
8	E. T. V. & G	36.06
7	L. & N.	36.11
6	L. S. & M. S.	37.27
5	C. & N. W	37.56
4	U. Pacif.	40.80
3	N.Pacif.	41.52
2	St.L. & San F.	41.88
1	St. P.M. & M.	46.08

10%   20%   30%   40%

it. It became the point where eastern lines met western lines (or at least midwestern lines). Gateways at St. Louis, Memphis, and New Orleans have enjoyed similar, albeit smaller, roles.

The importance of gateway cities is evident in railroad names (e.g., the New York, Chicago & St. Louis; the Minneapolis, St. Paul & Sault Ste. Marie; the Cincinnati, New Orleans & Texas Pacific) and in the ways that companies joined together. Railroad moguls planning systems via merger or other arrangements looked to reach key interchange points and tap major sources of traffic. However, railroads that did little more than connect the dots—reaching between gateways—eventually suffered if they didn't also develop lucrative online traffic. Known as bridge routes, they relied on their ability to bridge traffic between gateways. Although often sought as strategic routes in some mogul's grand scheme, these tended not to be the healthiest properties.

In the 1890s, PRR was America's busiest railroad. Its multiple track mainlines were accommodating a growing swell of freight and passenger traffic. This woodcut illustration from *The American Railway* depicts Mantua Junction in West Philadelphia, which helps put PRR's traffic in perspective. *The American Railway from 1893, Solomon collection*

EARLY-TWENTIETH-CENTURY GIANTS

By 1900, railroads were among America's largest and most powerful companies, and as America grew, traffic swelled and the network grew as well. The continued growth of railroads over eight decades led some railroad moguls to anticipate continued growth into the twentieth century, and they positioned their networks accordingly, building and acquiring lines to handle future traffic swells.

Philadelphia was focus of the Pennsylvania Railroad system; it served as the company headquarters with lines radiated out in every direction. PRR's Connecting Railway was built in the 1860s to allow for a through rail route between Philadelphia and the New York area. This 1908 postcard view depicts an eastward train crossing the Schuylkill River outbound from Philadelphia. *Solomon collection*

In his book, *American Railroad Transportation* (1910), Emory Johnson wrote that in 1907 more than 2,440 corporations owned railway lines in the United States, of which roughly 1,000 were operating companies. These provided railway service on an estimated 230,000 route miles consisting of 330,000 track miles. Despite the vastness of the network and the myriad companies involved, Johnson identified 17 regional systems representing the core of the American railroad system (excluding Canada), while further noting that the eight largest systems controlled two-thirds of American mileage. "Each [system represents a host of individual investors, but the control of the property of each group is centralized in the individual, or, at most, the few men standing at the head of the 'interest.'"

In the Northeast, the networks controlled by the Vanderbilts and Pennsylvania Railroad dominated both the map and traffic flows, while in the West, competing networks controlled by Edward H. Harriman and James J. Hill vied for supremacy. In the South, banker

Northern Pacific was the first northern transcontinental route and originally reached from Duluth, Minnesota, to Puget Sound via Bismarck, North Dakota, and Billings, Montana. By the early twentieth century it was among the railroads controlled by James J. Hill. This view portrays the testing of NP's truss bridge over the Missouri River at Bismarck. *The American Railway from 1893, Solomon collection*

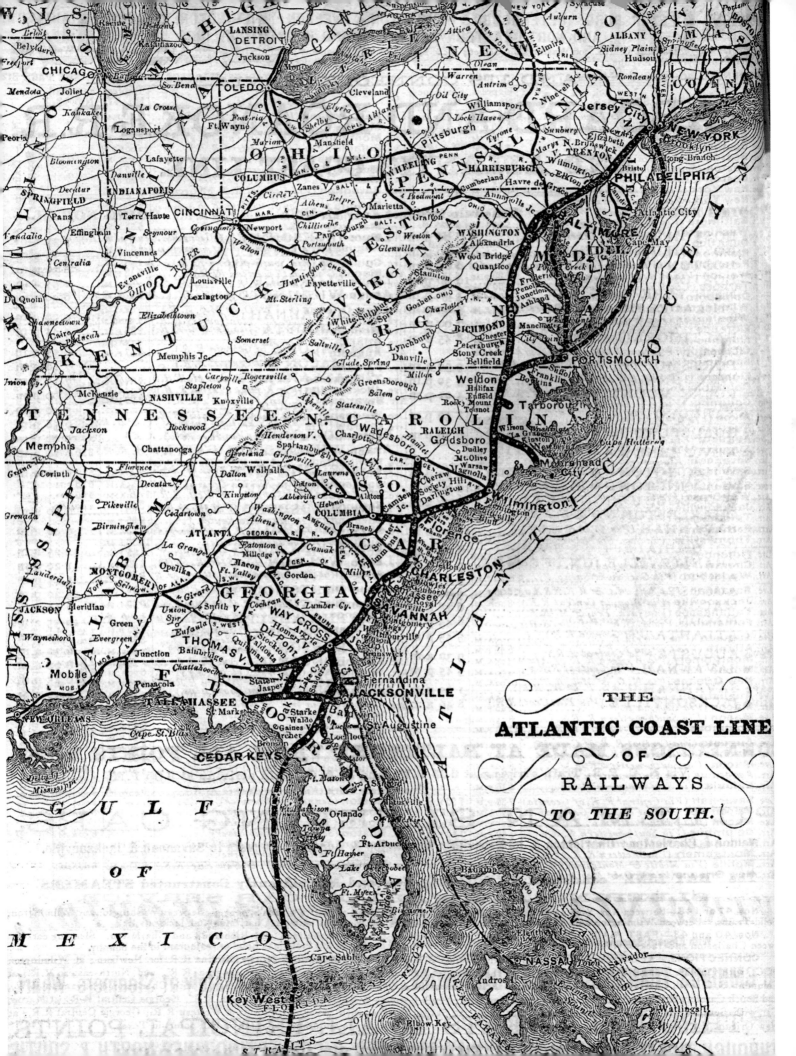

THE

ATLANTIC COAST LINE

OF

RAILWAYS

TO THE SOUTH.

The early twentieth century was a dynamic time for American railroads; traffic was booming and companies were consolidating to form massive transportation dynasties. New Haven railroad was among the New England lines controlled by Charles S. Mellen. Railroad crews work to expand the Worcester, Massachusetts, yard, which was a key gateway for interchanging freight with Mellen's Boston & Maine. *William Bullard photo, courtesy of Dennis Lebeau*

J. P. Morgan was dominant, though his influence was also evident on a variety of properties around the country. He was a primary backer of Hill and other regional railroad barons, among them Charles S. Mellen, who dominated New England through his control of the New Haven and Boston & Maine systems. The New England region was unusual because Mellen, with backing from Morgan, secured nearly a complete New England transport monopoly; not only did he systematically buy control of most of the northeastern railroads, but in Connecticut he had all of the streetcar and interurban electric lines and steamship companies as well. By 1911, his control across southern New England included half interest in Vanderbilt's leased Boston & Albany. Furthermore, Boston & Maine's lines covered most of New Hampshire and tapped strategic Vermont markets. Plus, B&M owned Maine Central. Canada's Grand Trunk Railway and its Central Vermont subsidiary offered the only real competition, and that was contained to just a couple of corridors.

Where Mellen dominated one region, George Gould looked to construct a true trans-continental system spanning the United States from Baltimore to San Francisco Bay. In 1892, Gould inherited a far-flung railroad empire from his father, the infamous Jay Gould and, in the twentieth century, added a variety of properties to his portfolio. Other early-twentieth-century systems included the south-central collection of railroads under the control of Benjamin Franklin Yoakum. Between 1896 and 1904, Yoakum gradually assumed control of the St. Louis & San Francisco (Frisco), which he used as the foundation for a group of roads connecting Chicago, St. Louis, and the Gulf of Mexico. In 1903, he took control of Chicago & Eastern Illinois while developing a close affiliation with Chicago, Rock Island & Pacific (Rock Island Lines), the large

Mellen System, 1903–1913

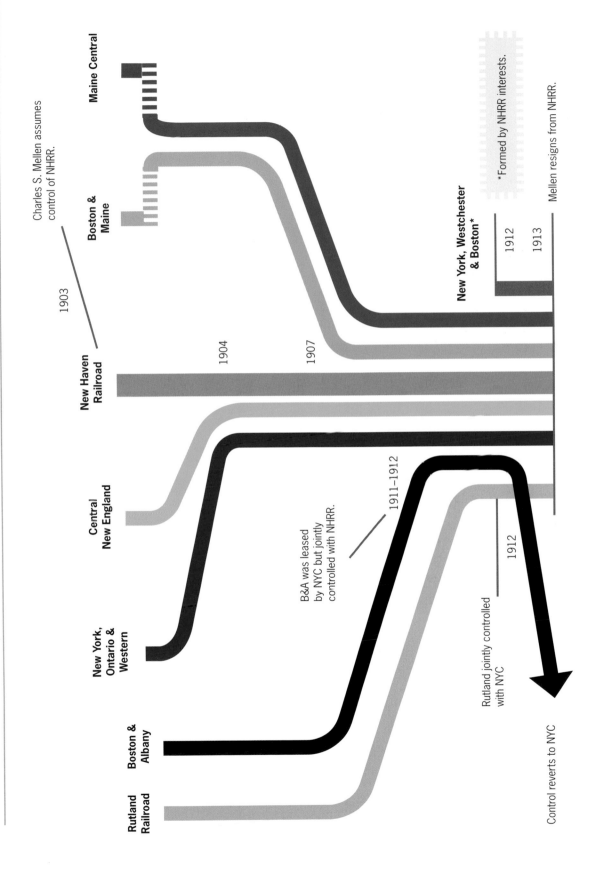

Maine Central

Boston & Maine

Charles S. Mellen assumes control of NHRR.

1903

New Haven Railroad

1904

1907

New York, Westchester & Boston*

1912

1913

Mellen resigns from NHRR.

*Formed by NHRR interests.

Central New England

New York, Ontario & Western

B&A was leased by NYC but jointly controlled with NHRR.

1911–1912

Boston & Albany

Rutland Railroad

Rutland jointly controlled with NYC

1912

Control reverts to NYC

Gould Railroads

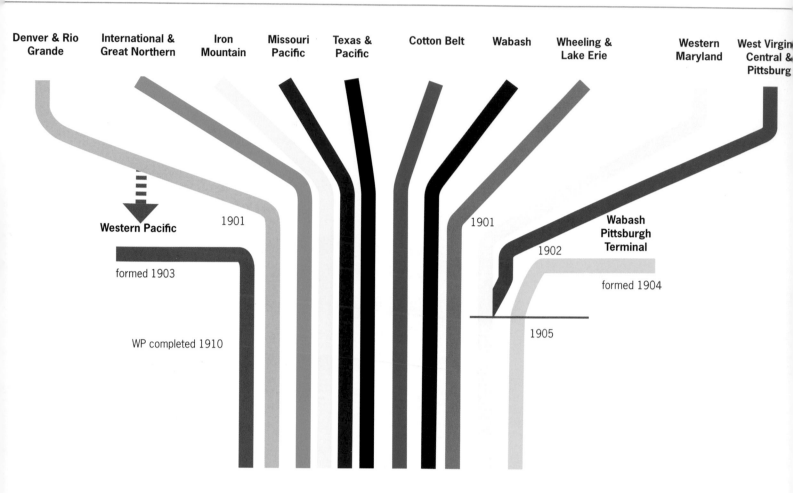

Denver & Rio Grande | International & Great Northern | Iron Mountain | Missouri Pacific | Texas & Pacific | Cotton Belt | Wabash | Wheeling & Lake Erie | Western Maryland | West Virginia Central & Pittsburg

Western Pacific

1901

formed 1903

WP completed 1910

1901

1902

Wabash Pittsburgh Terminal

formed 1904

1905

network partially controlled by the Reid-Moore Syndicate. Later, Yoakum founded the Gulf Coast Lines.

Meanwhile, Edwin Hawley, an erstwhile associate of the late Collis P. Huntington (one of the principals behind Central Pacific and Southern Pacific), assembled a network of midwestern lines, starting with the Minneapolis & St. Louis. During the first decade of the twentieth century, he created a group of lines that straddled the precarious gap between the Harriman and Hill systems and made forays east of the Mississippi.

Observing the trends of the times, Johnson wrote, "It seems probable that it will not be many years before the railroads of the United States as a whole will be divided into a small number of systems, each serving a well-defined territory, and each owned by a distinct group of capitalists." Yet, just the opposite occurred. By the time he penned those words, the trend toward mega systems had lost its momentum.

THE PENDULUM SWINGS

Railroad transportation benefited all Americans. Railroads made intercity travel cheaper, faster, and vastly more comfortable but also facilitated rapid industrial and agricultural growth, enabled the rapid settlement of western lands, and opened up massive exploitation of natural resources. Once the railroad boom was under way it was like, well, a runaway locomotive, gaining power with each piston stroke. Lines were built to every corner of the nation, with narrow gauge and lightly built electric interurban lines filling the gaps in mainline networks. Competitive forces often resulted in two or more railway companies serving prosperous points, sometimes on duplicate routes resulting in separate sets of tracks built side by side.

No one benefited more from railroads than their owners. By the end of the nineteenth century, the men who ran the railroad companies were among the wealthiest in the world. However, while the general public idolized the locomotive engineer, it had little admiration for the moguls, who were often vilified by the press. Decades of unregulated operations had resulted in numerous abuses of the public interest real and perceived. When train wrecks claimed lives by the dozens, the railroads were portrayed as monsters; when they extracted the highest rates possible from small shippers, they were decried as parasites living off the backs of honest men.

In the late nineteenth and early twentieth centuries, the movement toward massive corporate consolidation exacerbated negative public opinion, which ultimately fostered action by the federal government. Attempts in the late 1800s at regulating railroading, including creation of the Interstate Commerce Commission, hadn't resulted in effective government control. By contrast, more serious legislation enacted in the early 1900s changed the face of American transportation. While regulation wasn't limited to railroads, the reactive legislation enacted during the backlash against big corporations produced a devastating effect on private American railroading, resulting in a dramatic redrawing of the network map.

Key to this change was Hill and Harriman's battle for control of the Northwest, which reached a fevered pitch in 1901. Hill's empire was focused on his Great Northern transcontinental route, while Harriman had taken control of Union Pacific in 1897 and 1898 and assumed control of the sprawling Southern Pacific network. Hill's routes terminated at the Twin Cities, while Harriman's UP only reached as far east as Omaha. Both desired a friendly connection to Chicago. In 1901, Harriman attempted to trump Hill by surreptitiously taking stock control of the Burlington, a well-built, well-managed line in Hill's sphere of influence. Hill responded by securing full control of Burlington via its owner, Northern Pacific, by creating an enormous holding company called Northern Securities—a big a step toward Hill's consolidation of Great Northern, Northern Pacific, and Burlington into one super system. To placate his rival (amid cries of monopoly), Hill offered partial ownership of Northern Securities to Harriman. The move backfired, with long-standing consequences.

James J. Hill Railroads

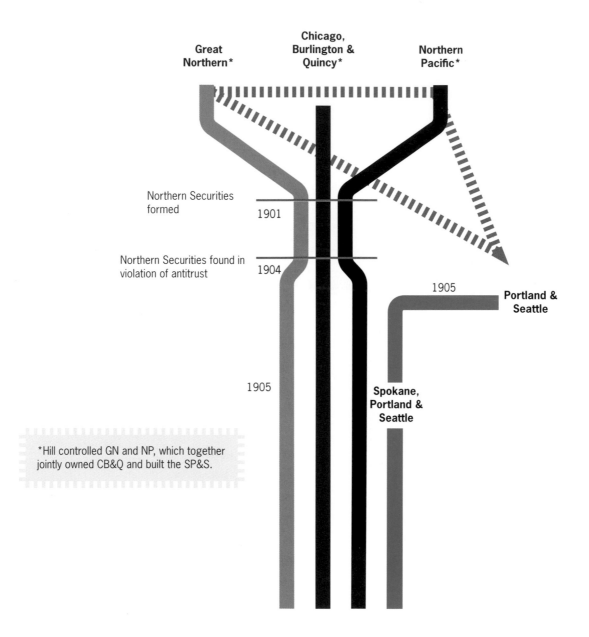

Great Northern*

Chicago, Burlington & Quincy*

Northern Pacific*

Northern Securities formed

1901

Northern Securities found in violation of antitrust

1904

1905

Portland & Seattle

1905

Spokane, Portland & Seattle

*Hill controlled GN and NP, which together jointly owned CB&Q and built the SP&S.

To outsiders, the Northern Securities consolidation and subsequent truce seemed like collusion. Public outrage sent lawmakers into action, and Northern Securities became the focus of President Theodore Roosevelt's crusade against big-business trusts. The Roosevelt administration prosecuted Northern Securities on antitrust grounds, and the Supreme Court upheld the government in 1904. This set a groundbreaking precedent that resulted in the breaking up of many railroad affiliations over the next decade, including Harriman's UP-SP combination.

CHANGING TIMES

There were other forces of change. Among these was passage of the Hepburn Act in 1906. Among other things, this legislation forced many railroads to divest control of industries for which they offered primary transport. Coal-hauling railroads were targeted. The anthracite lines that had become an unusually incestuous industry were the topic of close scrutiny.

Legislation was only part of the change. The caliber of men leading railroads underwent transformation. As regulation and competition brought the golden age of railroading to an end, it no longer attracted the most cunning and powerful men to lead it. More significantly, although perhaps less obviously, between 1906 and 1916 the generation of railroad titans that shaped the industry during its most influential decades died or were forced out of the business. Alexander Cassatt, the enlightened head of the Pennsylvania Railroad, died prematurely in 1906, leaving PRR's empire to less visionary men. Harriman died in 1909 on the eve of unparalleled federal scrutiny of his network. J. P. Morgan, the brilliant titan of American banking and a visionary force who had offered clarity and wisdom behind countless railroad schemes and reorganizations, died in 1913. And James J. Hill died in 1916. Known as the Empire Builder, Hill left his mark not just in exceptionally well-built railroads, but also in a generation of well-trained and well-groomed managers.

While time claimed many of railroading's most capable leaders, ripples in the economic fabric of business toppled others. It has been written that George Gould inherited his father's fortune and empire but not his father's exceptional business acumen. After 1900, Gould rapidly added a collection of second-tier railroads to his father's network while planning to fill gaps in his transcontinental vision by building new super railroads. The exceptional cost of late era construction was unsustainable. The financial earthquake that rocked business in 1907 ruined him. By 1908 his empire began to crumble, and by the onset of World War I, Gould was effectively out of railroading, his transcontinental aspirations unfulfilled.

Delaware, Lackawanna & Western's New York area terminals were at Hoboken, while Erie Railroad's were in adjacent Jersey City; both lines bored through the Palisades and crossed over one another on the west side as pictured in this 1893 image. *The American Railway from 1893, Solomon collection*

27

Baltimore & Ohio Expansion

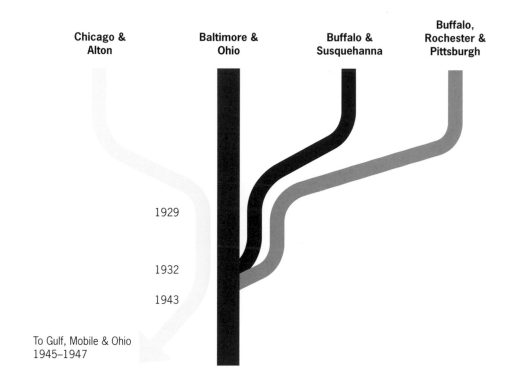

Mellen's New England network suffered from multiple hits as it reached its zenith. The 1913 death of its benefactor, J. P. Morgan, came just as the federal government moved to break up the network. Meanwhile, the Vanderbilts and the Pennsylvania Railroad aimed to avoid scrutiny by appearing to sever ties with affiliated lines or at least minimize their direct influence on these properties.

World War I brought unprecedented government control of railroads, and by the 1920s, the American map had changed. New affiliations and systems were taking hold. However, where railroads were virtually free from serious competition before World War I, by the 1920s they were faced with rapidly growing highway competition that benefited from massive government investment and a well-developed automotive industry that resulted from intensive wartime research and development.

Post–World War I realignment of railroads would produce some unpredictable combinations, and while some longtime railroad families would remain on friendly terms, new combinations would pit onetime allies against each other and pair old foes in curious ways.

Chapter 2

MARRIAGES OF CONVENIECE
Regulations, Competition & Realignment, 1916–1945

Changes between 1906 and 1920 produced unpredictable consequences for the railroad business and altered the very nature of American transportation. When several things change all at once, the results can be impossible to predict. Theodore Roosevelt's administration brought about an era of increased railroad regulation just as motorized highway transport was gaining a foothold. The side effects of antitrust legislation, specifically the Hepburn Act of 1906, curtailed railroads' potential profitability, thus limiting their ability to access capital. Further Supreme Court rulings and legislation restricted railroads' flexibility on rate structures. Starved of investment capital, railroads pared major expansion projects and slowed infrastructure improvements, effectively freezing the American network. The network ossified and, except for a handful of strategic connections, very few new routes were built after 1910.

Although traffic levels continued to swell, very little action was taken to increase network capacity or eliminate choke points. Meanwhile, further legislation in the form the Clayton Act of 1914, prevented railroads from directly controlling competing lines and encouraged railroads that had acquired competitors to spin them off, causing parasitic competition in which weak railroads siphoned traffic from healthier lines rather than allowing healthy lines to route traffic via friendly parallel connections. Hostile arrangements discouraged development of network connections as railroads aimed to fend off competitors. (The lack of effective track connections

In 1940, Lehigh Valley 4-8-4s moved tonnage. For a brief time in the mid-1920s, Lehigh Valley was part of a three-way affiliation with Delaware & Hudson and Wabash. When this combination fell apart, Pennsylvania Railroad picked up Lehigh and Wabash. *Jay Williams collection*

In its heyday, Delaware, Lackawanna & Western earned a fortune hauling anthracite; in its later years it developed its well-groomed low-grade mainline as a bridge route between the New York–metro area and Buffalo. *Solomon collection*

at junctions makes it difficult to utilize lines operated by different companies or routes built at different times. Thus, route structures don't always function as they might appear to on a map. Just because two lines cross, doesn't mean that they connect, and even if a connection exists, it may not facilitate easy interchange.)

As war heated up in Europe, American industries moved record amounts of tonnage and railroad traffic became acutely congested. Even before direct American military involvement in Europe, traffic had begun to congeal. Yards and interchange points were saturated as the network, suffering from a decade of underinvestment, boiled over from traffic.

By the end of 1917, the federal government had taken control of railroad operations, serving the role of traffic cop in rush-hour gridlock. For approximately two years, the United States Railroad Administration operated the majority of American railroads. Among the difficulties it faced were inadequate network connections between competing parallel lines that made it difficult to set up uni-directional traffic arrangements on parallel single-track lines so as to

emulate double-track. In a few situations the USRA made such improvements, notably in central Nevada where Southern Pacific and Western Pacific mainlines were converted to directional "paired track," allowing improved traffic flow on both routes.

USRA also addressed issues of locomotive design. Historically most railroads ordered small batches of custom-tailored machines. In an effort to benefit from a standardized parts supply, the USRA drafted a host of standard locomotive types suited for general operation across the American network.

World War I resulted in complex economic changes. Notably, it brought about a dramatic increase in labor costs, with railroad operations under the USRA experiencing notable rises. Not only were wages increased, but to facilitate movement of goods during wartime, the USRA dramatically increased the numbers of employees. When operations were returned to the private railroad companies in 1920, railroads were saddled with much higher labor costs than before the USRA had taken over. This proved especially troublesome for marginal operations, such as

Van Sweringen Railroads, 1916–1930s

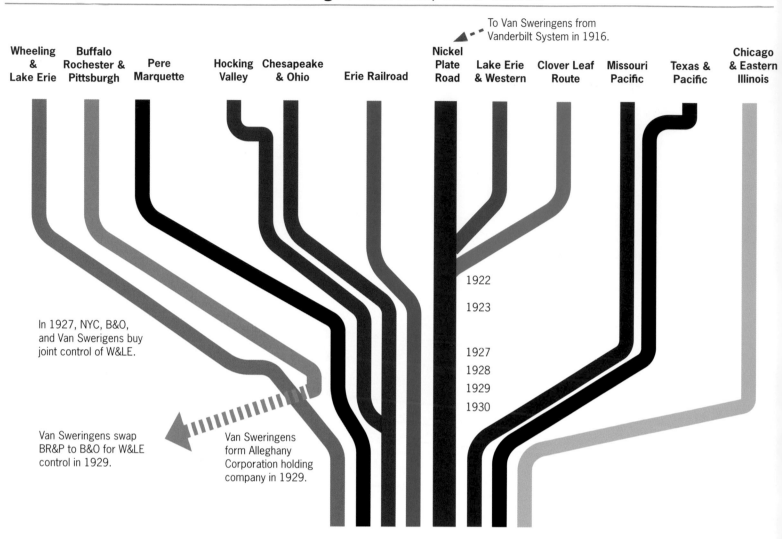

Wheeling & Lake Erie

Buffalo Rochester & Pittsburgh

Pere Marquette

Hocking Valley

Chesapeake & Ohio

Erie Railroad

Nickel Plate Road

Lake Erie & Western

Clover Leaf Route

Missouri Pacific

Texas & Pacific

Chicago & Eastern Illinois

To Van Sweringens from Vanderbilt System in 1916.

In 1927, NYC, B&O, and Van Swerigens buy joint control of W&LE.

Van Sweringens swap BR&P to B&O for W&LE control in 1929.

Van Sweringens form Alleghany Corporation holding company in 1929.

1922

1923

1927
1928
1929
1930

light branches where profits tended to be elusive and competition from highways had already claimed the most lucrative traffic.

Before the USRA returned railroad operations to the private companies there were calls for total railroad nationalization. This may have seemed an extreme solution but it was in line with world opinion. The United States proved a rare exception and retained private operations and control of infrastructure. By contrast, most world railway networks were under some form of government control by 1940.

The Transportation Act of 1920 further changed the railroad game. The ICC was given responsibility for overseeing railroad mergers, including planning for logical national consolidation of railroad companies. Neither the ICC nor the railroads embraced this edict enthusiastically. Although a general consensus noted too many railroad companies, solutions to the problem were controversial. So the ICC made master plans that had little hope of voluntary implementation while railroads pursued their own consolidation agendas. Among the better known ICC plans of the 1920s was William Z. Ripley's suggested merging of all the American lines into 24 systems.

VAN SWERINGEN EMPIRE

In this changed environment, several new systems and alliances took shape. Most significant was the railroad network developed by Cleveland-based entrepreneurs Oris P. and Mantis J. Van Sweringen, eccentric brothers whose style involved highly leveraged control via complex financing and intricate holding companies. Initially, New York Central president Alfred H. Smith, who found the Van Sweringens suitable allies in his plan to safely divest of the Nickel Plate Road in 1916, supported the brothers' plans. The Nickel Plate connected Buffalo and Chicago via Cleveland, running parallel to New York Central's Water Level Route. While Central needed to unload the Nickel Plate to fulfill mandates of the Clayton Act, it hoped to do so in a way that facilitated a friendly competitor rather than hostile competition, such as handing the line to one of its traditional foes such as the Pennsylvania Railroad.

Working behind the scenes with the New York Central, the Van Sweringens expanded Nickel Plate's reach by merging it with the Clover Leaf Route and Lake Erie & Western. Next, they began an aggressive plan of acquisition and in 1923 took control of the Chesapeake & Ohio system, followed by the Erie Railroad and the Pere Marquette in 1924.

An Erie Railroad 0-8-0 switcher crosses the railroad's Newark Branch bascule bridge over the Passiac River. Had the Van Sweringen brothers been allowed, they would have assembled one of the most powerful railroad networks in America, reaching from the East Coast to Chicago and St. Louis and to the Gulf of Mexico, as well as routes in the heart of bituminous coal country and Canada's Ontario province. *Richard H. Young*

Cleveland's New Railway Terminal Is G-E Equipped

THIS great $60,000,000 station marks the latest advance in the electrification of union passenger terminals in America. It will be opened early in 1930.

Seven railway lines, all heavy passenger carriers, converge at Cleveland. Only an electrified terminal could carry the daily thousands of travelers to and from the heart of the city—with the necessary speed and convenience and with the comfort and smoothness demanded of modern railways.

Twenty giant electric locomotives, each eighty feet long and each able to haul seventeen

75-ton Pullman cars, will be supplied with power by five 4000-hp. motor-generator sets. A single operator in the passenger station automatically controls the two power substations miles away.

All these new electric locomotives carry the General Electric monogram. So do the big motor-generator sets. So does the floodlighting system, which gives special distinction to the terminal tower. The same General Electric mark of dependability is also found on thousands of other electric products, such as MAZDA lamps and electric refrigerators,—home necessities which promote health and comfort.

JOIN US IN THE GENERAL ELECTRIC HOUR, BROADCAST EVERY SATURDAY AT 9 P.M., E.S.T. ON A NATION-WIDE N.B.C. NETWORK

The Van Sweringen legacy included construction of Cleveland Union Terminal with its iconic Terminal Tower, as featured in this 1930 General Electric advertisement. *Buck collection*

The Van Sweringen lines established a joint motive power design called the Advisory Mechanical Committee with the Vans' lieutenant John J. Bernet in charge of procuring the best standard designs. Bernet encouraged the design of 2-8-4s. So successful was that type that Nickel Plate continued to buy new 2-8-4s for more than a decade after the Vans had passed from the scene. Nickel Plate 740 leads a freight at Rocky River, Ohio in June 1948. *J. William Vigrass*

Smith died suddenly in 1924, just as the Van Sweringens were reaching the apex of their influence. Their relations with New York Central began to cool. While the Van Sweringen railroads benefited from a common motive power policy based on modern "super power" designs offered by Lima, the railroads maintained individual identities. The brothers planned to merge Nickel Plate, Erie, C&O, and Pere Marquette into a unified trunk system, but it was not to be; despite proclamations promoting consolidation, in 1926 the ICC vetoed Van Sweringens' merger plans. The brothers responded by setting up their Alleghany [*sic*] Corporation as a holding company and then continued to add railroads to their portfolio.

Notably, they acquired interest in the Wheeling & Lake Erie jointly with B&O and Central while snapping up the Buffalo, Rochester & Pittsburgh at about the same time. Then, in a peculiar transaction in 1929, they effectively swapped the BR&P for B&O's share of the Wheeling. In 1930 they shifted their focus west, picking up the former Gould linchpin, Missouri Pacific, and then the Chicago & Eastern Illinois a short time later. C&EI gave the MP system access to the Chicago gateway and offered a key link in their growing collection of railroads.

The Van Sweringen empire was poised to become a transcontinental route when its finances unraveled during the Great Depression. The brothers died in 1935 and 1936, by

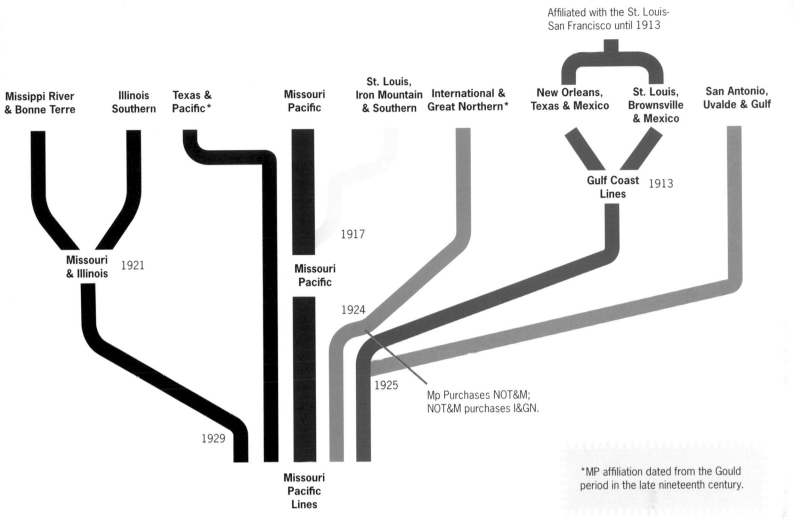

Affiliated with the St. Louis-
San Francisco until 1913

Missippi River
& Bonne Terre

Illinois
Southern

Texas &
Pacific*

Missouri
Pacific

St. Louis,
Iron Mountain
& Southern

International &
Great Northern*

New Orleans,
Texas & Mexico

St. Louis,
Brownsville
& Mexico

San Antonio,
Uvalde & Gulf

Gulf Coast
Lines   1913

1917

Missouri
& Illinois   1921

Missouri
Pacific

1924

1925

Mp Purchases NOT&M;
NOT&M purchases I&GN.

1929

Missouri
Pacific
Lines

*MP affiliation dated from the Gould
period in the late nineteenth century.

which time they were ruined financially. However, their Alleghany Corporation continued to exert influence on railroad combinations long after their deaths, and some of the affiliations they established in the 1920s and 1930s carried on into the megamerger era of the late twentieth century. Furthermore, their infrastructure improvements, such as Cleveland Union Terminal, including the Shaker Heights rapid transit lines, continued to benefit railroads for decades.

D&H STAKES OUT A FIFTH SYSTEM

An almost-forgotten episode of 1920s railroad posturing was the bold effort by Delaware & Hudson president Leonor Loree to carve out a "fifth system." Where the Van Sweringens served as New York Central's proxy, Loree reacted to the Van Sweringens' empire building by working with Pennsylvania Railroad's tacit blessing.

Historically, the four major eastern east-west trunk lines had been New York Central, Erie Railroad, Pennsylvania Railroad, and Baltimore & Ohio. Of these, NYC and PRR were roughly matched, while Erie was decidedly the weak sister. This seemed likely to change if the Van

Delaware Hudson's "Fifth System"

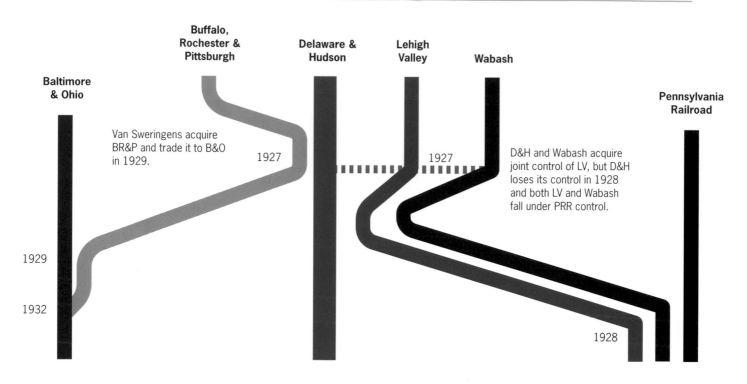

Baltimore & Ohio

Buffalo, Rochester & Pittsburgh

Delaware & Hudson

Lehigh Valley

Wabash

Pennsylvania Railroad

Van Sweringens acquire BR&P and trade it to B&O in 1929.

1927

1927

D&H and Wabash acquire joint control of LV, but D&H loses its control in 1928 and both LV and Wabash fall under PRR control.

1929

1932

1928

Sweringen consolidation plan came to fruition—the Erie combined with C&O, Nickel Plate, and the other roads represented a strong combination. In response, Loree, in combination with the Wabash, acquired control of Lehigh Valley in 1927 and, on its own D&H, leased Buffalo, Rochester & Pittsburgh between 1925 and 1927.

The D&H–Lehigh Valley–Wabash network connected major eastern gateways, but its route structure was haphazard and offered no real competition to other trunks. However, this was only part of Loree's original scheme. He'd anticipated acquisition of Wheeling & Lake Erie and Western Maryland, and planned to build an ambitious new east-west low-grade trunk across Pennsylvania. Loree's ambitions flew in the face of established interests, resulting in a tide of opposition and a lack of support—not even PRR was keen on the low-grade line, which would have run parallel to its own mainline. Loree's dream fell apart and in 1928 PRR picked up the pieces, inheriting control of both Lehigh Valley and Wabash while Loree and D&H continued separately. Ironically, a few years later, B&O (of which Loree had been president when PRR controlled the line) briefly revived the low-grade concept, again to no avail. Today, Interstate 80 follows the approximate route of the proposed Pennsylvania low-grade.

BALTIMORE & OHIO EXTENDS ITS REACH

At the turn of the twentieth century, Baltimore & Ohio had been under the yoke of its rival, the all-powerful Pennsylvania Railroad. PRR began to ease control by 1906, by which time B&O controlled the Reading Company (and thus Central Railroad of New Jersey, which had long been

Spheres of Influence, 1900–1912

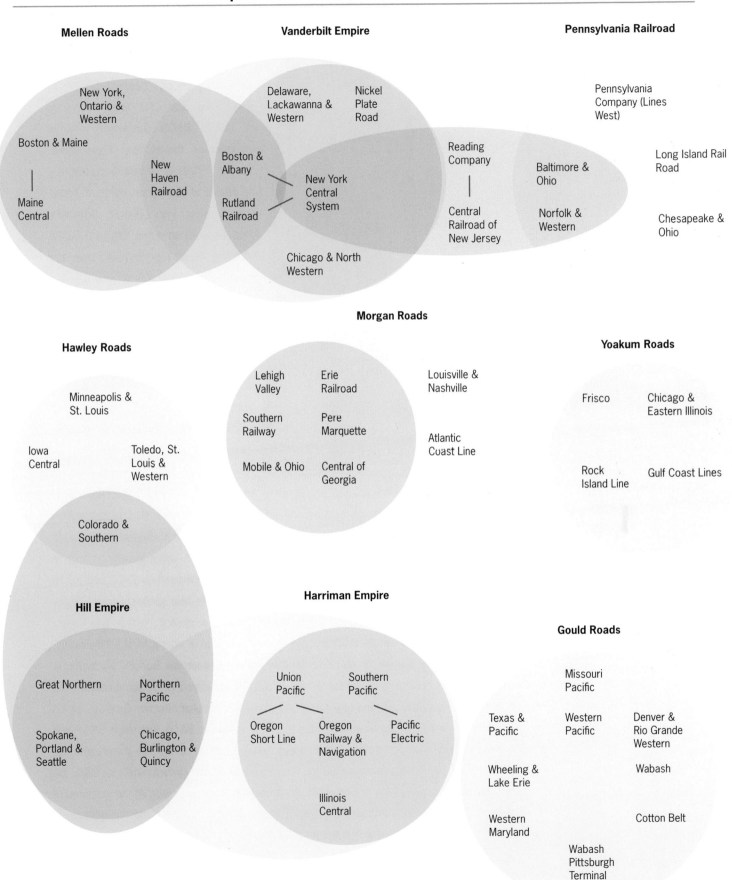

Mellen Roads

New York, Ontario & Western

Boston & Maine

Maine Central

New Haven Railroad

Vanderbilt Empire

Delaware, Lackawanna & Western

Nickel Plate Road

Boston & Albany

Rutland Railroad

New York Central System

Chicago & North Western

Reading Company

Central Railroad of New Jersey

Baltimore & Ohio

Norfolk & Western

Pennsylvania Railroad

Pennsylvania Company (Lines West)

Long Island Rail Road

Chesapeake & Ohio

Morgan Roads

Hawley Roads

Minneapolis & St. Louis

Iowa Central

Toledo, St. Louis & Western

Lehigh Valley

Erie Railroad

Southern Railway

Pere Marquette

Mobile & Ohio

Central of Georgia

Louisville & Nashville

Atlantic Coast Line

Yoakum Roads

Frisco

Chicago & Eastern Illinois

Rock Island Line

Gulf Coast Lines

Colorado & Southern

Hill Empire

Great Northern

Northern Pacific

Spokane, Portland & Seattle

Chicago, Burlington & Quincy

Harriman Empire

Union Pacific

Southern Pacific

Oregon Short Line

Oregon Railway & Navigation

Pacific Electric

Illinois Central

Gould Roads

Missouri Pacific

Texas & Pacific

Western Pacific

Denver & Rio Grande Western

Wheeling & Lake Erie

Wabash

Western Maryland

Cotton Belt

Wabash Pittsburgh Terminal

TIME TABLES

GULF MOBILE AND OHIO
RAILROAD

GULF MOBILE AND OHIO
RAILROAD

The Rebel Route

The South's First Streamlined Air Conditioned Trains
JANUARY 2, 1941

The South's First Streamlined Air Conditioned Trains
JANUARY 2, 1941

This colorful January 1941 Gulf, Mobile & Ohio public timetable radiates optimism. GM&O was formed through merger of Isaac B. Tigrett's Gulf, Mobile & Northern and Mobile & Ohio. After World War II, it expanded by acquisition of the Alton route from Baltimore & Ohio. GM&O formed a north-south network roughly parallel to Illinois Central. *Solomon collection*

in Reading's camp). B&O's control was evident in its through passenger services over Reading and CNJ lines to Jersey City. (While B&O's passenger services terminated on the Hudson River shore, from the 1920s it offered a connecting bus service to Manhattan points to better compete with Pennsylvania Railroad's direct services to Penn Station. B&O's freight to New York traveled over the Staten Island Rapid Transit and reached Manhattan using car ferries.)

In 1910, Daniel Willard took B&O's helm as president. A lifelong railroader and protégé of James J. Hill, Willard immediately began extending B&O's reach. In 1910, he improved B&O Chicago connections through acquisition of the Chicago Terminal & Transfer Railroad, which was transformed into a subsidiary, Baltimore & Ohio Chicago Terminal (a line that continued to operate its own equipment into the diesel era). B&O's midwestern connections were improved with purchase of the Cincinnati, Hamilton & Dayton in 1916.

In the 1920s Willard took ICC's consolidation plans to heart, using the opportunity to expand B&O further. It acquired the Cincinnati, Indianapolis & Western in 1927 and jointly acquired the Wheeling & Lake Erie about the same time while also gaining control of the Western Maryland. (The ICC frowned on B&O's direct control of WM, which was largely parallel to its route, and forced B&O to hold its WM stock in a voting trust.) Meanwhile, in 1929, B&O traded control of W&LE to the Van Sweringens for the Buffalo, Rochester & Pittsburg while also taking control of the Buffalo & Susquehanna around the same time. At first glance, these Pennsylvania-based coal roads seem to offer a peculiar direction for B&O, which had largely focused expansionist efforts in the Midwest. However, B&O's interest in BR&P and B&S wasn't just for their coal traffic. Rather, it was part of a plan to build a low-grade east-west trunk across central Pennsylvania toward the New York metro area. Unfortunately for B&O, the Great Depression quashed any hopes of obtaining financing for the project. At the west end of its system, B&O acquired the financially weak Chicago & Alton line but shed this addition in the 1940s, ultimately conveying it to the expanding Gulf, Mobile & Ohio system.

Formation of Gulf, Mobile & Ohio, 1917–1947

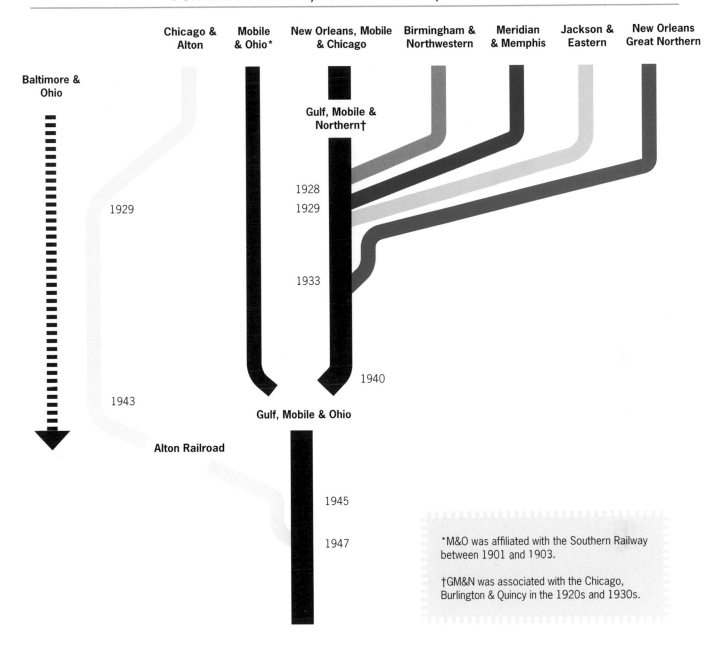

Chicago & Alton — Mobile & Ohio* — New Orleans, Mobile & Chicago — Birmingham & Northwestern — Meridian & Memphis — Jackson & Eastern — New Orleans Great Northern

Baltimore & Ohio

Gulf, Mobile & Northern†

1929
1928
1929
1933
1943
1940

Gulf, Mobile & Ohio

Alton Railroad

1945
1947

*M&O was affiliated with the Southern Railway between 1901 and 1903.

†GM&N was associated with the Chicago, Burlington & Quincy in the 1920s and 1930s.

GULF, MOBILE & OHIO EKES OUT A PLACE

GM&O was the post–World War I creation of Isaac B. Tigrett, who rapidly eked out space on the map. Tigrett assumed the presidency of GM&O antecedent Gulf, Mobile & Northern during the USRA period era. GM&N itself was a late-era railroad that had emerged from the ashes of the failed New Orleans, Mobile & Chicago. During the 1920s (after USRA control ended), Tigrett aggressively expanded GM&N by assuming control of key connecting short lines: Birmingham & Northwestern in 1924, Jackson & Eastern in 1927, and the strategically important New Orleans Great Northern between 1929 and 1933. More significant expansion occurred in the late 1930s when GM&O was formed as a vehicle to facilitate the 1940 merger of GM&N with one-time Southern Railway affiliate Mobile & Ohio, creating GM&O.

Southern Pacific Aquisitions, 1924–1932

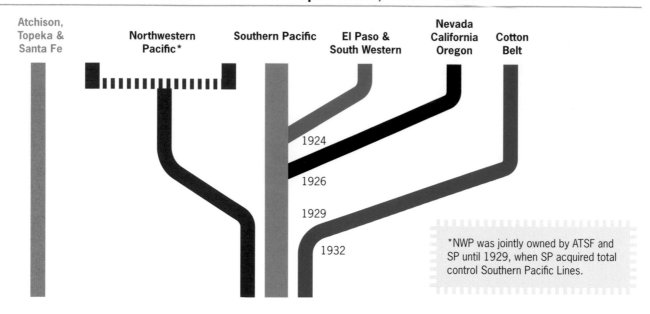

Atchison, Topeka & Santa Fe

Northwestern Pacific*

Southern Pacific

El Paso & South Western

Nevada California Oregon

Cotton Belt

1924

1926

1929

1932

*NWP was jointly owned by ATSF and SP until 1929, when SP acquired total control Southern Pacific Lines.

After World War II, GM&O acquired the Alton route from B&O, finally merging with the line in 1947. Significantly, GM&O never bought a new steam locomotive and, in 1949, was among the first large railroads to achieve total dieselization.

SOUTHERN PACIFIC OFFENSIVE AND DEFENSIVE ACQUISITIONS

Following Edward Harriman's death in 1909, Southern Pacific faced a decade of grueling and complex legal battles. First, the courts separated it from Union Pacific and then made an unsuccessful attempt to untangle Central Pacific from Southern Pacific. By the mid-1920s, with these trials behind, SP embarked on a series of acquisitions and heavy construction projects.

In 1924, with the ICC's blessing, SP acquired the El Paso & South Western system. This regional system extended west along the Mexican border to Tucson, Arizona, and had several significant branches, including a line into northern Mexico. Notably, EP&SW gave SP a direct connection with Rock Island at Tucumcari, New Mexico, cementing this eastward gateway promoted by SP as its Golden State Route—an important move for SP, considering its recent split from UP—while giving SP added capacity on the Sunset Route. Perhaps, more importantly, SP prevented EP&SW from developing as a competing route to southern California, since much of its line was roughly parallel to SP's Sunset Route. And in addition to its vital Rock Island connections, EP&SW also connected with Texas & Pacific at El Paso.

In 1926, SP completed its highly engineered Natron Cutoff, providing a vastly superior route between northern California and Oregon, supplanting SP's sinuous and heavily graded Siskiyou Line. Then in 1929, SP opened its Alturas Cutoff (known in later days as its Modoc Line), a 251-mile route that connected with SP's east-west Overland Route at Fernley, Nevada, and ran geographically northwest via Alturas, California, to a connection with the Natron Cutoff near Klamath Falls, Oregon. To secure a route for the Alturas Cutoff, in 1926 SP had taken

A Southern Pacific freight works the Alturas Cutoff. This was one of the last through routes completed in the steam era; SP assembled it through purchase and regauging of the narrow gauge Nevada-California-Oregon and construction of connections from its Overland Route on the east end Natron Cutoff on the west end. This desert shortcut saved SP freight heading toward Oregon hundreds of miles of mountain running. *John E. Pickett*

After George Gould's empire unraveled, Denver & Rio Grande Western, Western Pacific, and Missouri Pacific maintained a loose family relationship. While D&RGW's standard gauge mainlines conveyed transcontinental traffic, its three-foot gauge lines continued to serve local customers at high elevations. In time-honored tradition, a narrow gauge Mikado works the Monach Branch at Garfield, Colorado. *John E. Pickett*

Western Pacific Expansion, 1916–1929

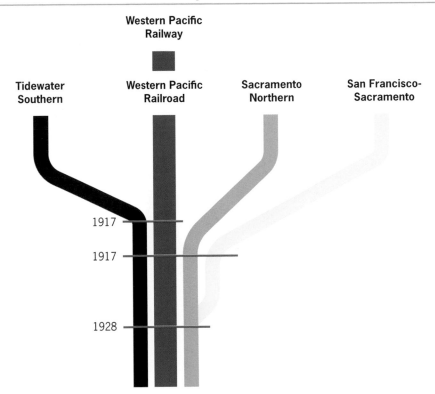

**Western Pacific
Railway**

**Tidewater
Southern**

**Western Pacific
Railroad**

**Sacramento
Northern**

**San Francisco-
Sacramento**

1917

1917

1928

control of the narrow gauge Nevada-California-Oregon line that operated on a north-south alignment between Reno, Nevada, and Lakeview, Oregon, via Alturas. Both of SP's late-era cutoffs involved considerable major new construction and were among the last new routes in the West completed during the steam era.

Since the early twentieth century, SP and the Santa Fe Railway had jointly owned the Northwestern Pacific. NWP reached from marine terminals, across the bay from San Francisco, through California's Marin County, northward through the timber producing regions of Mendocino and Humboldt counties, to Eureka on the northern California coast. In 1929, SP bought out Santa Fe's interest in NWP, which it continued to operate as a subsidiary with equipment and operations retaining the NWP identity.

SP's boldest post–World War I expansion, however, was its 1932 acquisition of the St. Louis Southwestern (commonly known as the Cotton Belt), a route that had floundered after George Gould's empire unraveled. Cotton Belt gave the SP access to the important Memphis and St. Louis gateways and important sources of traffic in Arkansas and eastern Texas. SP allowed Cotton Belt a high degree of autonomy; its locomotives and equipment continued to be lettered for the line into the 1990s.

WESTERN PACIFIC EXPANDS

Among the strategic flaws in George Gould's transcontinental railroad planning was a lack of feeders bringing traffic to his new mainlines. It was as if he'd done little more than connect the dots on a map. This was especially problematic for his Western Pacific, which spanned

Formation of Canadian National Railways, 1917–1923

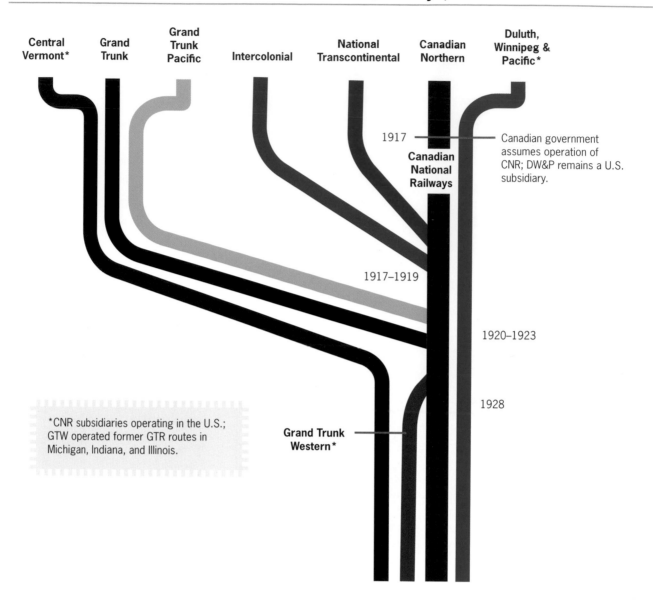

Central Vermont* Grand Trunk Grand Trunk Pacific Intercolonial National Transcontinental Canadian Northern Duluth, Winnipeg & Pacific*

1917 — Canadian government assumes operation of CNR; DW&P remains a U.S. subsidiary.

Canadian National Railways

1917–1919

1920–1923

1928

*CNR subsidiaries operating in the U.S.; GTW operated former GTR routes in Michigan, Indiana, and Illinois.

Grand Trunk Western*

800 miles across some of the most remote and barren country in the United States to reach the port of Oakland, California. While WP passed through California's fertile Central Valley and connected Sacramento and Stockton, it had virtually no branches with which to gather traffic. In 1916, its reorganization resulted in Gould's Western Pacific Railway giving way to the Western Pacific Railroad, a company jointly owned by Denver & Rio Grande Western and Missouri Pacific.

Western Pacific Railroad immediately set out to correct the deficiencies of its predecessor and, in 1917, acquired the Tidewater Southern, an interurban electric line operating in the agriculturally rich area between Stockton, Modesto, and Turlock. In 1921, WP acquired Sacramento Northern, another electric line, which it merged with the San Francisco–Sacramento Railroad to form an all-electric alternative route between the Bay Area and California's capital, with lines extending northward through the Central Valley to Fairfield, Marysville, and

Yuba City. WP operated these electric lines as subsidiaries.

In the late 1920s, WP built a new line north from its mainline at Keddie, California, to Bieber where it met a newly constructed branch of the Great Northern system to create the California-Oregon freight corridor, known as the Inside Gateway, that competed with SP's Cascade Route. By offering connections with the Santa Fe at Stockton, WP served as part of an alternate north-south route between the Pacific Northwest, Southern California, and points east that completely bypassed SP and UP systems.

CANADIAN NATIONAL SURVIVES UNDER GOVERNMENT CONTROL

During the early years of the twentieth century, privately financed Canadian railways embarked on a variety overly ambitious expansion schemes. By 1915, key railroad companies were floundering and Canada was faced with supporting its unprofitable yet necessary railroads. The situation was by no means unique to Canada—in many countries railroads were in a similar situation.

Initially, unprofitable companies were operated by the Canadian Government Railways. As more lines required attention, the Canadian National Railway (CNR) was formed about 1918. First to join were the National Transcontinental and Intercolonial railways. Then CNR assumed operation of the extensive Canadian Northern system, including its American subsidiary, Duluth, Winnipeg & Pacific. Canada's Grand Trunk Railway and its far-flung Grand Trunk Pacific subsidiary refrained from joining CNR immediately but, by 1921, were unsustainable and finally merged into CNR in 1923. Grand Trunk's American lines, including Central Vermont Railway, retained a degree of independence under CNR control, yet were very much part of the Canadian National family. In 1928, CNR set up the Grand Trunk Western Railway to operate former Grand Trunk Railway lines in Illinois, Indiana, and Michigan. Not all Canadian railways were amalgamated into the CNR system; notably, the Canadian Pacific Railway remained private and continued to thrive in competition with CNR.

Cover of the joint Grand Trunk/ Canadian National Railways June 1942 public timetable. Grand Trunk was Canadian National Railway's largest American subsidiary. *Solomon collection*

Chapter 3

FIXED MARRIAGES

Merger Machinations and Maneuvering
in the Cold War Era, 1945–1976

The years 1945 through the 1970s were some of the most tumultuous times in the modern history of American railroading. Wide-scale adoption of new technologies combined with revised labor practices, increased modal competition (highways, airlines, and water-based transport), and drastic changes in traffic patterns. Waves of railroad mergers changed the railroads' corporate structures and business models while erasing traditional names and routes from the map. Some mergers were well planned and proved successful; others were unmitigated disasters. Although railroads were slow to pursue major consolidations after World War II, by the late 1950s the entire industry was buzzing with merger talk with more than 30 combinations discussed. More than a dozen significant mergers had been implemented by the mid-1970s.

Mergers can be viewed in several categories. Merging railroads were typically either parallel or end-to-end. They could be independent or affiliated while serving as either competitors or friendly connections. With parallel mergers, companies shared common territory and enjoyed similar traffic while often serving many of the same major customers and reaching the same gateways and major cities. With end-to-end mergers, railroads connected at gateways and tended to augment each other's territory and thus complement one another. Historically, regulatory bodies favored end-to-end mergers, while parallel consolidations were viewed as reducing competition and bad for the public interest.

Pennsylvania Railroad was the most powerful railroad in the East and the largest freight hauler. This 1951 advertisement stresses the enormity of its postwar investment in new freight cars. *Solomon collection*

200 MILES of NEW FREIGHT CARS

Biggest Freight Car Order in Railroad History!

Twenty Thousand New All-Steel Freight Cars... enough to form one solid train extending from New York to Baltimore and beyond!

Just what industry is calling for as production speeds up everywhere   8,250 box cars, 11,500 gondolas, 250 flat cars   an increase of 5,000 cars since our last report.

Several thousands of these new cars are already in service. Eleven thousand will have been completed and put to work by March 31 The balance will come

along at an average of a thousand a month. Freight car builders say this is by far the largest car order ever placed by one railroad. These 20,000 cars will cost $114 million, making a total of $133 million the Pennsylvania Railroad will have spent for newer and better freight cars since January, 1950.

This order to car builders will expand the Pennsylvania Railroad's vast freight fleet to keep pace with the growing demand for railroad transportation by industry and defense.

PENNSYLVANIA RAILROAD
Go by Train...Safely—with Speed and Comfort

During the Chessie System era, Western Maryland was integrated with B&O in stages. In 1977, a westward WM freight works the B&O mainline at Meyersdale, Pennsylvania. It passed below WM's Cumberland-Connellsville mainline that was downgraded following hurricane damage in the mid-1970s. *George W. Kowanski*

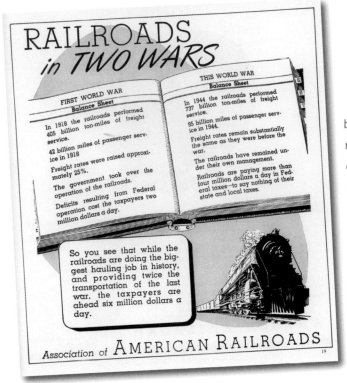

This 1945 advertisement stressed the superior wartime performance of American railroads under private management, more than just a subtle reminder at a time when most railway systems in the world were under national control. *Solomon collection*

Although hundreds of individual railroad names were on the books, beginning in the mid-nineteenth century many American railroads were linked through various means, including leases, degrees of stock control, interlocking directorships, and holding companies. Some affiliations produced clear family-like relationships, others were less obvious and invisible in day-to-day operations. Golden age affiliations put lines into spheres of influence that evolved over the years as fluctuations in national and world economies shaped the roots of business and industry.

World War II was a high-water mark for American railroad traffic. Into the early 1950s railroads retained high volumes of freight and passenger traffic, offering renewed optimism following the difficult years of the Great Depression. During this time of relative prosperity there was minimal interest in mergers; instead most lines focused on investing in new technology, bringing physical plants back up to prior standards following deferred wartime maintenance, and replacing fleets of worn-out equipment. Flashy new streamlined diesels and lightweight passenger trains were the face of postwar railroading, yet railroads also invested in modern pushbutton centralized traffic control signaling, massive modern classification yards, radio communications, and new varieties of freight cars. This improved efficiency made individual employees more productive while simplifying operations.

POSTWAR MERGERS

There were few minor consolidations in the immediate postwar period. In 1947, three mergers made news. Denver & Rio Grande Western absorbed Denver & Salt Lake, a natural consolidation that was barely noticed by the industry. Completion of DSL's Moffat Tunnel in the late 1920s, combined with D&RGW's construction of the Dotsero Cutoff, had offered the most recent transcontinental link through the Rockies west from Denver.

More significant was Gulf, Mobile & Ohio, itself a recent creation, merging with the Alton. Until 1945, the Alton was part of the Baltimore & Ohio system, connecting Chicago, St. Louis, and Kansas City. The Alton gave GM&O the link it needed to form a through route from the Gulf Coast to Chicago.

Also in 1947 was the merger of Pere Marquette and Chesapeake & Ohio, which had a close affiliation since the mid-1920s as parts of the Van Sweringen empire. After the empire collapsed, its affiliations unraveled. When a proposed unification of former Van Sweringen lines fell apart after World War II, C&O and Nickel Plate Road parted ways. On a map, the C&O and PM systems may seem to have had little in common, but PM offered C&O valuable Michigan-based auto traffic while providing important access to markets and gateways for

C&O's bituminous coal traffic, their lifeblood. PM retained an element of independence in the C&O system for few years but was gradually assimilated.

While interested railroads occasionally broached merger, for the most part railroads concentrated on completing dieselization and major capital projects. A decade passed before another major consolidation took place.

THE CURSE OF INTERESTING TIMES

In the 1950s, the tide turned against the industry. While railroads had faced competition from highways since World War I, World War II had partially reversed the trend. But by the mid-1950s increased public highway investment (immensely expanded with Eisenhower's Interstate Highway System) seriously cut into railroad profits. Improved roads and growing car ownership devastated long-distance passenger business (despite the railroads' massive investments in postwar streamliners), which suffered from growing annual deficits. A far more serious problem stemmed from trucking, which rapidly skimmed away lucrative high-value and time-sensitive freight business. Furthermore, new industries that developed had an alarming highway-based focus that left railroads out in the cold. Most railroads couldn't afford to construct routes to tap new traffic and had to be content with a route structure that dated from an earlier era. Economic changes dating from World War I made it progressively more difficult for railroads to finance new construction.

Compounding matters were government regulation and legislation that perpetuated antiquated and rigid rate structures and obsolete labor arrangements while making it difficult for railroads to discontinue unprofitable services or introduce competitive innovation. Furthermore, railroads faced high taxes on their privately funded infrastructure while governments clung to obsolete attitudes from the railroads' golden age and continued to view them as monopolistic giants of transport.

Hardest hit were railroads serving the northeastern states where rapid declines in anthracite coal (traditionally one of the most lucrative revenue streams) and the loss of railroad-friendly heavy industries combined with heavy commuter rail losses and traffic erosion from short-haul trucking. Another threat was the opening of the St. Lawrence Seaway in the late 1950s, which captured low-value bulk traffic. Railroads' efforts at diversification into other modes had been largely squashed on anticompetition grounds in the 1920s and 1930s, and while intermodal operations in the form of piggyback (trailer-on-flatcar) had been liberalized in 1954, these were still strictly regulated, greatly limiting railroad intermodal services. Recessions in the late 1950s compounded the problems for weak railroads. In this desperate climate, consolidation seemed to be the best solution.

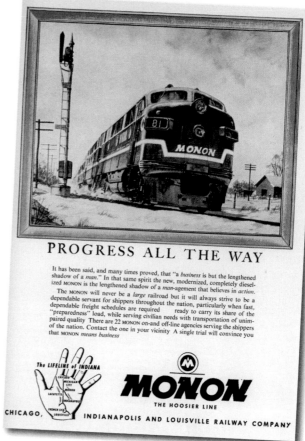

After World War II, Monon was transformed into a lean modern railroad by the administration of John W. Barriger, which invested in new diesels and freight cars while improving passenger service. This ad is from 1951, a full two decades before the line was absorbed by Louisville & Nashville. *Solomon collection*

MERGER MAGIC

Traffic declines since the end of World War II combined with productivity gains that allowed fewer trains to carry more traffic resulted in excess capacity. In short, railroads were maintaining more infrastructure than they needed to move existing volumes of traffic. In the 1950s and early 1960s, railroads viewed mergers as the best means to restore competitiveness by lowering costs, improving productivity, minimizing competition, and eliminating duplicate infrastructure. Railroads believed that concentrating traffic on fewer lines would result in savings through economies of scale. By lowering costs, railroads would gain efficiency and be more competitive. Serious highway competition rendered old arguments against reducing railroad competition through merger irrelevant.

Historically, railroads had complained that the glacial pace of the Interstate Commerce Commission (ICC) had impeded merger proposals. What was the point of commissioning studies to evaluate savings and other merger advantages, and wasting years of valuable management time and energy in the process, if after a prolonged review a merger proposal was declined?

No merger proposal was viewed in isolation. When any railroad suggested a combination, the entire industry scrutinized the proposal in detail. Would this new combination hurt existing traffic? Might it pave the way for more mergers? Should conditions be demanded? As the ICC began approving mergers in the late 1950s, and conditions facing railroads became more acute, the merger movement rapidly gained momentum. Whereas the "M word" was hardly used in the railroad trade press in 1950, by the end of the decade it was *the* talk of the industry.

It was a difficult and tedious process to bring a merger to fruition. If a friendly merger was proposed, management quietly broached the topic with their intended partner. Secrecy was paramount: the railroad industry has been described as an "information sieve," with details of changes spreading rapidly among the ranks. Since high finance was involved, if a whisper of merger got out too soon, stock prices would rise, and competing interests would soon look to derail the process or demand conditions, either of which would drive up the price of consolidation.

When managements agreed, they would seek studies to justify their actions while obtaining approval of stockholders and preparing proposals to the ICC seeking regulatory approval. Mergers of the 1950s and 1960s were based on lowering costs through labor reductions, diverted traffic, and other changes affecting shippers and communities along the lines. As a result, mergers had to be carefully explained in order to avoid excessive complaints. Railroads approached affected parties, including unions, shippers, and competitors with proposals to placate concerns, while soliciting support from anyone who might lend it. In a complicated merger, the process might take years with no guarantee of success. If railroad management was careless they might give away too much too soon and thus offset benefits of merger through concessions to opposing parties. If they were too conservative the process might die on the vine or be condemned by the ICC.

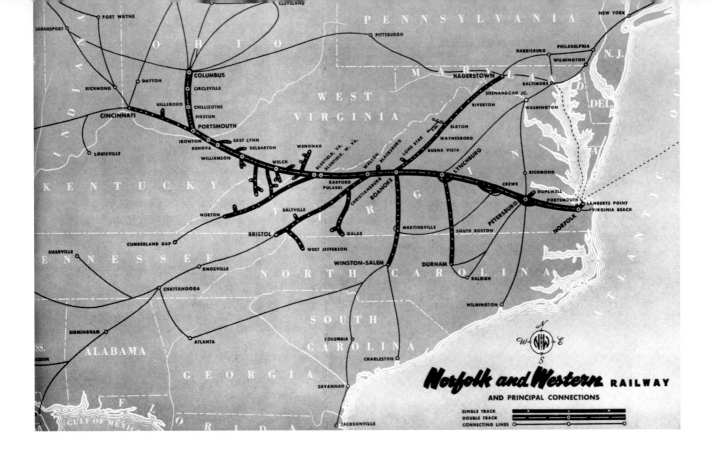

TRENDSETTING ACTIONS

After a decade without a major merger, ICC approved the merger of the Louisville & Nashville with the Nashville, Chattanooga & St. Louis. The latter had been controlled by L&N since the 1880s, and while this consolidation essentially took place within the same family, it was of considerable interest to the industry. Richard Saunders highlighted its significance in his 1978 book, *Railroad Mergers and the Coming of Conrail*, explaining that it was the first merger to assert savings through retrenchment. The speed of approval was likewise significant; the railroads publicly agreed to merge in November 1954, submitted their proposal to the ICC two months later, and despite a litany of protests, received ICC approval on March 1, 1957.

Earlier merger rumors tended to involve relatively minor consolidations. But in 1956, the Hill Lines (Burlington, Great Northern, Northern Pacific, and affiliates) revived their plans for merger. This wasn't an earth-shattering proposition—in fact, it was their fourth effort at consolidation. The big story occurred in November 1957, when Pennsylvania (PRR) and New York Central (NYC) sent waves through the industry when it became public that they were in merger talks. Unlike the familial consolidations previously discussed, PRR plus NYC represented a massive parallel combination between historical archrivals. Not only were these America's two largest railroads in terms of traffic, but they also represented the core transportation empires around which Eastern railroading revolved. The event precipitated an avalanche of merger discussion, proposals, and reactive strategy.

In the meantime, the Transportation Act of 1958 aimed to provide railroads relief from the postwar economic and demographic changes by offering loan guarantees (primarily for

Continued on page 58.

A 1957 map of the traditional Norfolk & Western before its merger-era expansion that resulted in its acquisition of Virginian, Nickel Plate Road, Wabash, Pittsburgh & West Virginia and other roads. N&W remains a core route of today's Norfolk Southern. *Solomon collection*

Norfolk & Western Expansion 1959–1982

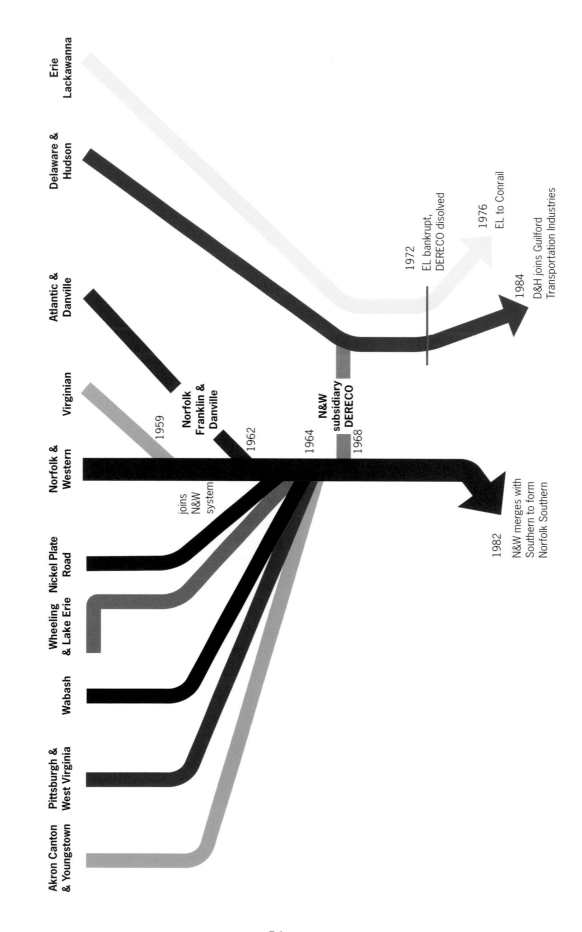

Akron Canton & Youngstown

Pittsburgh & West Virginia

Wabash

Wheeling & Lake Erie

Nickel Plate Road

joins N&W system

Norfolk & Western

Virginian

1959

Atlantic & Danville

Norfolk Franklin & Danville

1962

Delaware & Hudson

Erie Lackawanna

1964

N&W subsidiary DERECO

1968

1972
EL bankrupt, DERECO disolved

1976
EL to Conrail

1984
D&H joins Guilford Transportation Industries

1982
N&W merges with Southern to form Norfolk Southern

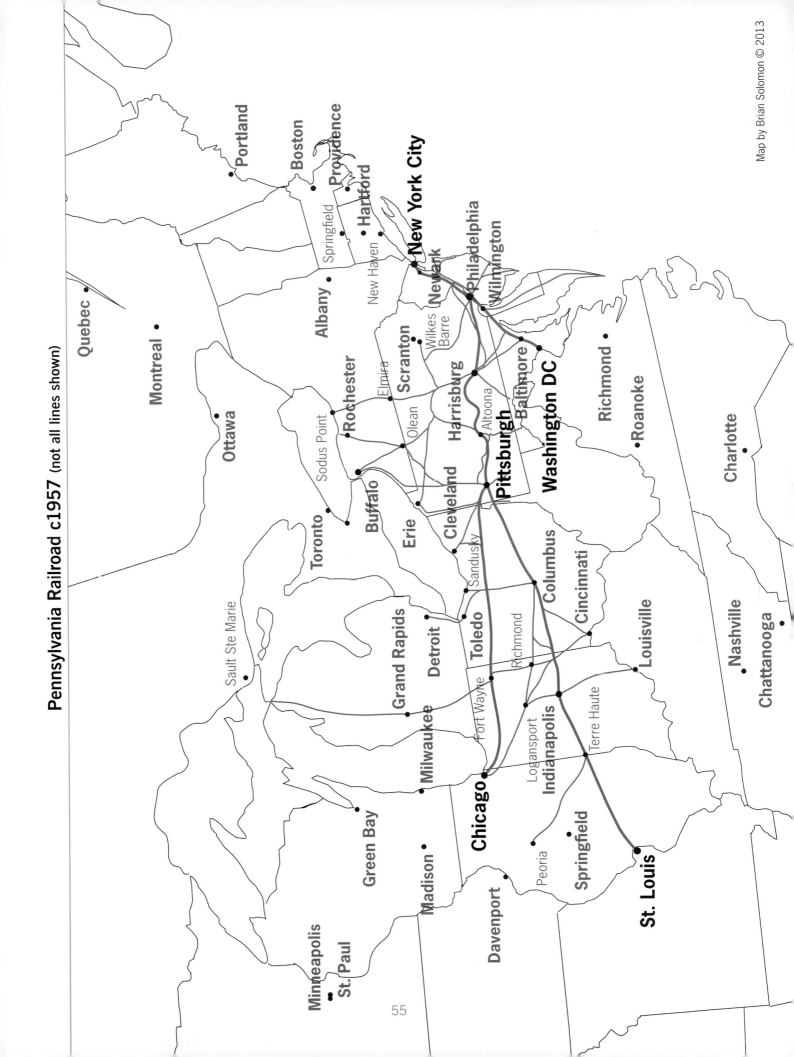

Pennsylvania Railroad c1957 (not all lines shown)

Map by Brian Solomon © 2013

55

Railway Age noted in 1958 that 86 percent of Virginian's revenue was from coal and coke traffic. Among the proposed benefits of the Virginian merger with N&W was the efficient blending the railroads' parallel routes, which included adapting Virginian's line east of Roanoke as a unidirectional low-grade coal funnel. However this didn't suit continuation of Virginian's high-voltage electrification, which N&W abandoned in 1962. *Richard J. Solomon*

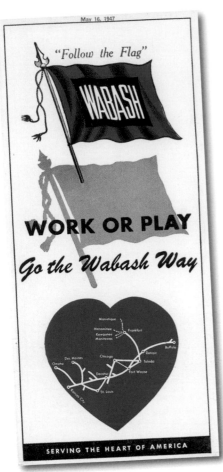

May 16, 1947

"Follow the Flag"

WABASH

WORK OR PLAY

Go the Wabash Way

SERVING THE HEART OF AMERICA

Although Wabash was a Pennsylvania Railroad satellite, it maintained a distinct appearance and independent operation while nothing in its public literature gave away its affiliation. *Solomon collection*

Continued from page 53.

deferred maintenance) and nominal rate relief, and easing the problems associated with growing passenger deficits by making it easier to discontinue underutilized trains and establishing precedents to encourage government subsidy for loss-making suburban services.

NORFOLK & WESTERN EXPANSION

In 1959, coal-rich Norfolk & Western moved to expand its system. It was one of the best run railroads in the East and the last major American line to begin the switch from steam to diesel power. More significantly, N&W was in Pennsylvania Railroad's sphere of influence. N&W's president and the mover behind its merger strategy, Stuart Saunders, was also a director of PRR. On December 1, N&W merged with the Virginian (a coal hauler directly parallel to N&W's mainline), resulting in a 2,750-mile network. Despite the parallel combination of profitable unaffiliated lines, the N&W–Virginian merger faced little opposition. The ink was barely dry on ICC approval when N&W began integration of the Virginian network to make connections between the two networks and lengthen the Virginian's sidings to 200-car capacity.

Encouraged by its success, on March 18, 1960, N&W announced plans to merge with Nickel Plate Road (known by reporting marks NKP). On the surface, this seemed a peculiar combination since it neither had historical precedent (NKP had been in the New York Central sphere; N&W in PRR's), nor was it a parallel or end-to-end combination. The two railroads shared no common points—quite simply, they didn't connect to one another. However, the gap was rectified when PRR sold its 111-mile north-south route between Columbus and Sandusky, Ohio, connecting the two systems and giving N&W a coal conduit to the Great Lakes (a route on par with C&O's Hocking Valley route obtained decades earlier). PRR approved the Sandusky line sale in autumn 1960, and not long after the N&W–NKP union was suggested, N&W added PRR's Wabash affiliate to its plan. Unlike many railroads in the East, N&W was profitable, which made its expansion significant. Ultimately, the three-way merger was approved by the ICC, though it was laden with caveats related to the renewed proposal between New York Central and PRR, wherein PRR had to divest its interest in N&W and control of Wabash.

The N&W–NKP–Wabash merger was consummated in 1964 whereby N&W bought NKP and leased Wabash from PRR. N&W also acquired NKP affiliate Wheeling & Lake Erie and the Canton, Akron & Youngstown and Pittsburgh & West Virginia. (W&LE and P&WV were remnants of George Gould's ill-fated attempt at a unified transcontinental and, in recent years, had served alongside the NKP as part of the Alphabet Route that competed with the major trunk lines for through traffic.)

N&W's rapid growth, combined with the continued PRR–NYC planning, spurred a variety of consolidation talks. Delaware & Hudson and recently created Erie-Lackawanna demanded inclusion in N&W's network because they feared being frozen out of friendly connections if

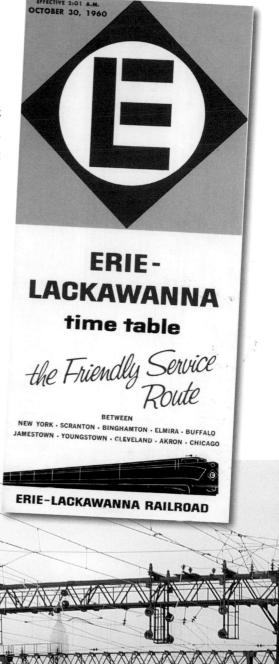

surrounded by the proposed Penn Central juggernaut. EL was viewed as a weak railroad and D&H wasn't much better, so N&W wasn't keen on absorbing these lines. Only after a few years of legal wrangling did N&W acquiesce to taking them on, but only by creating a subsidiary called Dereco (a name drawn from the initials of the acquired railroads) to shield it from potential losses.

THE ILL-FATED ERIE LACKAWANNA

Anthracite coal–haulers Delaware, Lackawanna & Western and Erie Railroad were historic competitors in the New York–Binghamton–Buffalo corridor. DL&W was a riches-to-rags case. Started as an Erie feeder, its lines were built to Erie's nonstandard six-foot gauge. Later in the nineteenth century, it shook its Erie ties and emerged as a leading anthracite carrier, expanding east and west from its base at Scranton, Pennsylvania. By the dawn of the twentieth century it was among the most prosperous lines in the East and made intensive investment in its mainlines, including high-profile, low-grade line relocations with massive reinforced concrete viaducts allowing it to improve its coal-hauling capacity while honing its mainline

In 1954, Delaware, Lackawanna & Western and Erie Railroad agreed on significant consolidation prior to initiating formal merger talks. Among the changes was Erie phasing out its Jersey City Terminal in favor of Lackawanna's expansive Hoboken facilities. *Richard Jay Solomon*

In June 1966, an Erie Lackawanna car float navigates New York Harbor. The lack of direct rail-freight connections between New Jersey to New York City resulted in extensive trans-Hudson car-ferry operations. Modern highway tunnels and bridges combined with a shift toward containerization have given road transport an economic advantage over car floats in the New York market. *Richard Jay Solomon*

as a bridge route between New York and Buffalo. By the end of World War II, DL&W's fortunes had waned. Anthracite was in steep decline and the line suffered from a rising passenger deficit tied to its intensive Hoboken, New Jersey–based suburban service. To survive, DL&W vied for bridge traffic with four other major routes.

The Erie Railroad had always been marginal. Of the four principal East Coast–Chicago trunk lines, Erie's was the weakest. And unlike New York Central and Pennsylvania Railroad, Erie's mainline missed almost every major metropolitan area between New York and Chicago, tapping major traffic sources with branches, feeders, and connecting lines. Earlier efforts at integrating Erie into a stronger network had failed.

In the late 1940s, DL&W approached Nickel Plate Road about a merger but was rebuffed. The two lines appeared a logical union, but NKP wasn't interested, partly because of DL&W's declining financial condition. Then, in the mid-1950s, DL&W and Erie cooperated in mutually beneficial physical consolidation, allowing both lines to eliminate redundant trackage: DL&W downgraded and abandoned portions of its double-track mainline between Binghamton and Corning, New York, in favor of Erie's adjacent line while Erie phased out its Jersey City passenger terminal, shifting its services to DL&W's underutilized and nearby Hoboken terminal.

These moves, combined with financial pressures imposed by the late-1950s recession, led to three-way merger discussions between Erie, DL&W, and Delaware & Hudson. The more prosperous D&H pulled out of discussions, but Erie and DL&W agreed to merge. They put their petition to the ICC in July 1959, and after detailed consideration, ICC approved merger in September 1960. Erie-Lackawanna was formed in October (the hyphen was dropped in the mid-1960s). This 3,188-mile system was proclaimed the largest merger of the twentieth century to date and seemed to herald a new era for eastern railroads.

Unfortunately for EL the root causes of its predecessors' losses hadn't been addressed. While consultants had estimated millions in annual savings, the new railroad was unable to substantially reduce costs. EL was nearly bankrupt a few years after it began. One-time DL&W president William White was brought on board in 1963 and temporarily reversed EL's fortunes. Later, when it faltered again, the company was brought into the N&W fold under that railroad's Dereco subsidiary.

EL benefited from N&W's strong connections at Buffalo, including joint investment in Bison Yard, and also from modern N&W-style motive power acquisitions. But Dereco proved short-lived. Following damage from Hurricane Agnes in 1972, EL declared bankruptcy and N&W dissolved the holding company. EL hoped to reorganize or find a suitable merger partner; instead, in April 1976, it was incorporated into the government-sponsored Conrail bailout.

BUILDING TO THE CHESSIE SYSTEM

Chesapeake & Ohio was among the healthiest railroads in the East. It enjoyed robust coal traffic, and though it operated a loss-making long-distance passenger service, the operation wasn't as intensive as on other roads, nor was C&O saddled with commuter services. In spring 1960, C&O entered merger talks with B&O, which had faced serious losses as result of the late-1950s recession. Both its traffic and finances were declining.

The situation became complicated following a temporary breakdown of the Pennsylvania Railroad–New York Central merger talks. NYC forced negotiations with B&O and C&O, hoping for a three-way merger. While B&O openly entertained both lines, C&O's emphasis was on a union with B&O (although *Railway Age* noted in its May 16, 1960, issue that C&O had also entertained merger discussions with Chicago & Eastern Illinois, Chicago & North Western, and

Continued on page 64.

This joint Chesapeake & Ohio/Baltimore & Ohio passenger timetable dates from 1969. C&O had used the "Chessie" nickname informally for decades, but in 1973, Chessie System was adopted as the trade name for C&O controlled railroads. *Solomon collection*

On February 21, 1975, Erie Lackawanna SD45-2 3676 roars east along New York's Canisteo River 309 miles from Jersey City. Hurricane Agnes caused raging flood waters that devastated many miles of E-L mainline, including this vulnerable section along the Canisteo, that precipitated the railroad's bankruptcy and resulted in its inclusion in Conrail. *Doug Eisele*

Continued from page 61.

Milwaukee Road, among others). C&O, cool to New York Central's proposal, moved to formally acquire B&O, resulting in a short-lived struggle with NYC. Ultimately, NYC backed off and resumed more fruitful merger discussions with PRR.

ICC approved C&O's control of B&O in December 1962, while C&O also bought an interest in Western Maryland which, combined with B&O's longstanding stock in the line, eventually led to C&O-B&O control of the WM.

The B&O-C&O route structures were complementary rather than parallel, and although they served a few common gateways, such as Washington, D.C., Buffalo, Cincinnati, and Chicago, their traffic flows were considerably different. As a result, the C&O-B&O merger was viewed as an end-to-end union and consolidation offered very few opportunities to reduce plant or blend operations. Benefits for B&O included C&O's progressive management and access to capital. Because WM was largely parallel to B&O, considerable consolidation took place between the two routes in the 1970s.

In their first decade of union, the B&O, C&O, and WM continued as largely independent operations and maintained individual identities, although B&O and C&O were involved in joint marketing and adopted similar paint liveries that emphasized dark blue with gold striping. This changed in 1973 when C&O formed Chessie System as a holding company for the three railroads and introduced a bright new paint scheme. Equipment continued to be sublettered for individual railroads, and B&O and C&O operations continued to be largely independent. During the Chessie System years, WM was integrated into B&O, and in the 1970s, WM mainlines west of its yard at Hagerstown, Maryland, were downgraded or abandoned in favor of B&O routes. In 1982, WM was formally merged into B&O.

SOO UPRISING

For decades, Canadian Pacific Railway's subsidiaries in the upper Midwest—Minneapolis, St. Paul & Sault Ste. Marie, Wisconsin Central, and Duluth, South Shore & Atlantic—enjoyed a family arrangement while maintaining some degree of independent operations. For many years MStP & SSM and Wisconsin Central were jointly operated as the Soo Line, connecting Chicago with Duluth, the Twin Cities, and CPR lines via international gateways at Sault Ste. Marie, Michigan; Noyes, Minnesota; and Portal, North Dakota.

In 1959, CPR commissioned a study to consider savings from merger of these affiliates, and in 1960, ICC approved CPR's proposal. In a confusing move, MStP & SSM and Wisconsin Central were merged into the DSS&A, which was then renamed the Soo Line Railroad. To promote this consolidation, Soo Line introduced a new modern livery and logo. While the Soo Line was essentially a consolidation of affiliated lines, it permitted some retrenchment as some of DSS&A's routes were downgraded or abandoned and shop facilities consolidated.

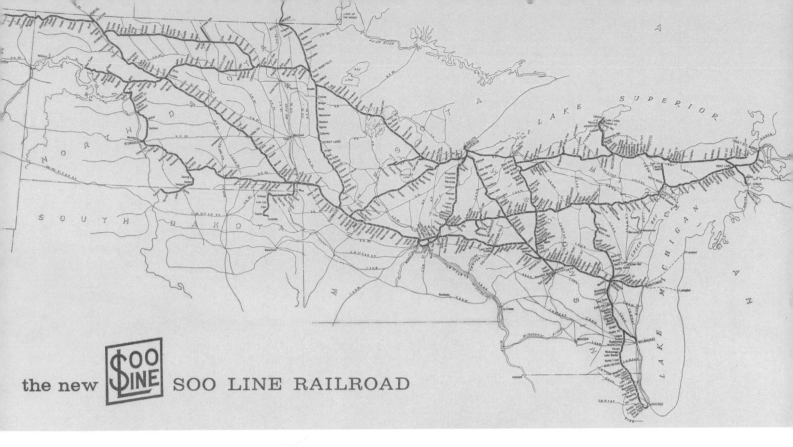

the new **$OO $INE** SOO LINE RAILROAD

FORMATION OF FAMILY LINES IN THE SOUTH

Seaboard Air Line and Atlantic Coast Line were largely parallel systems, connecting Washington, D.C. (via the Richmond, Fredericksburg & Potomac line to Richmond, Virginia), with the Carolinas, Georgia, and Florida. ACL operated a largely double-track route, while SAL's line was primarily single-track. Although SAL had suffered losses during the Great Depression, by the 1950s both railroads were healthy and enjoying robust traffic.

In 1958, the two lines began merger studies, and in July 1960, directors of the railroads filed with the ICC. SAL-ACL was viewed as an unorthodox union because the two railroads had a duplicate route structure, yet benefited from solid traffic bases and were healthy companies with relatively little rail competition. Still, the proposed merger moved forward on the premise that a single strong railroad could better maintain traffic under threat from other modes and be more capable of serving the public by retaining the railroad's competitive role.

This union was more than just a merger between two parallel lines: ACL had enjoyed a complex family relationship with the Louisville & Nashville system. Not only did ACL's holding company also control L&N, but together ACL and L&N controlled several railroads, including the Clinchfield Railroad in Georgia and the West Point Route (Atlanta & West Point and Western Railway of Alabama). The merger faced considerable opposition, not just from other railroads but also from labor, shippers, and communities along the lines. Nevertheless, it was approved by the ICC, and after a few last-minute hurdles, Seaboard Coast Line was formed in 1967.

L&N extended its reach to Chicago in 1969 through its acquisition of former Chicago & Eastern Illinois routes (L&N and Missouri Pacific had vied for control of C&EI in the early 1960s, ultimately deciding to divide the railway, with MP selling to L&N the eastern portion

Map of the newly formed Soo Line Railroad in its first year— 1961. *Solomon collection*

65

Seaboard System

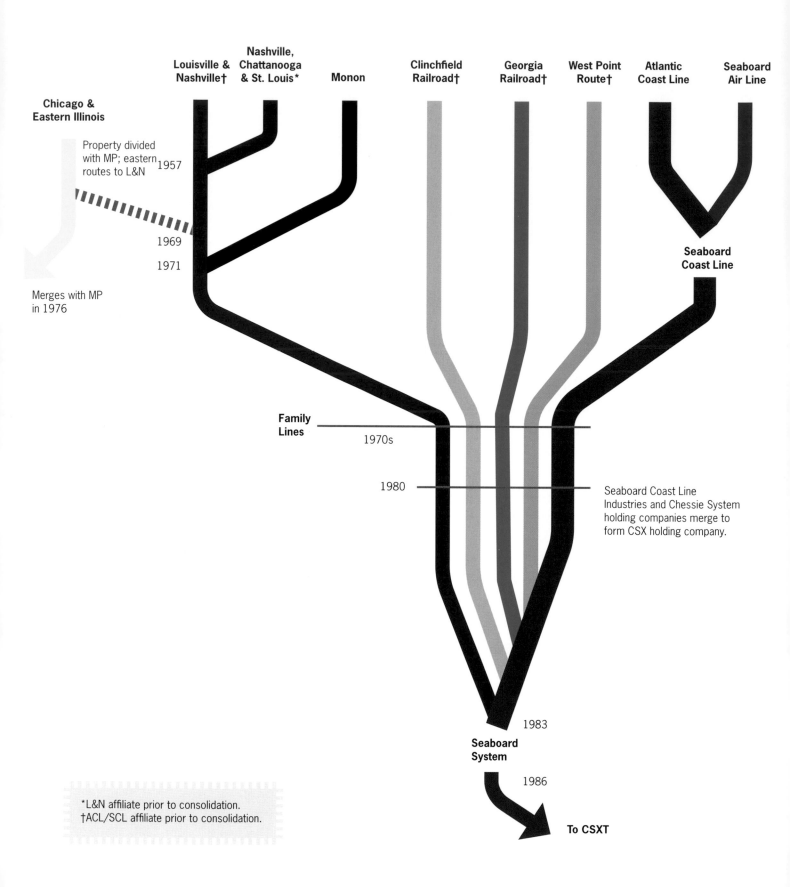

Nashville, Chattanooga & St. Louis*

Louisville & Nashville†

Monon

Clinchfield Railroad†

Georgia Railroad†

West Point Route†

Atlantic Coast Line

Seaboard Air Line

Chicago & Eastern Illinois

Property divided with MP; eastern routes to L&N 1957

1969

1971

Merges with MP in 1976

Seaboard Coast Line

Family Lines

1970s

1980

Seaboard Coast Line Industries and Chessie System holding companies merge to form CSX holding company.

1983

Seaboard System

1986

To CSXT

*L&N affiliate prior to consolidation.
†ACL/SCL affiliate prior to consolidation.

plus vital trackage rights). This provided L&N a through route from Louisville to Chicago; the line between Woodland, Illinois, and Chicago was used by both railroads. (C&EI was officially merged into MP in 1975.) In 1971, L&N tapped another Chicago route with its acquisition of the Monon, a railroad in which it had held part ownership decades earlier.

By the 1970s, SCL's holding company, Seaboard Coast Line Industries, began to jointly market its various railroads as the Family Lines, offering a simplified appearance for the complex (and seemly incestuous) relationships among the component railroads. Although locomotives and freight cars initially wore the Family Lines badge and the corporate structure was simplified, railroads continued to operate largely as independents. Consolidation of the Family Lines railroad began in 1981 and ultimately resulted in creation of the Seaboard System in 1983.

CHICAGO & NORTH WESTERN'S ACQUISITIONS AND ABANDONMENTS

Chicago & North Western was one of the so-called granger railroads, and its name aptly described the territory it served. The C&NW network included the Chicago, St. Paul, Minneapolis & Omaha, a line that it had controlled since the 1880s. While the so-called Omaha Road retained an element of independence in the steam era (with equipment sublettered for the line), after dieselization it was quietly absorbed by its parent (officially leased in 1957 and merged in 1972).

C&NW faced competition from myriad lines because its territories overlapped those of the Soo Line, Milwaukee Road, Burlington, and Rock Island. Among its most important routes was its Chicago–Omaha mainline. While favored by Union Pacific for transcontinental traffic, this was just one of six mainlines in the corridor. Beginning with Ben Heineman's management in the 1950s, C&NW initiated a series of mergers with smaller lines within its territory to secure greater traffic and minimize competition. First was the Litchfield & Madison, a central Illinois short line absorbed in 1958 to provide C&NW access to the St. Louis gateway. Heineman had come from the Minneapolis & St. Louis, a small well-liked and well-run line connecting the Twin Cities and the Peoria gateway, which was neatly absorbed by C&NW in 1960. Next was Chicago Great Western, a 1,411-mile network with principal lines reaching from Chicago to Omaha and from the Twin Cities to Kansas City via Des Moines. Soo Line had discussed merger with CGW in 1963, but in 1964 C&NW made the move, and in 1967 the merger was approved.

The October 24, 1960, *Railway Age* reported that the ICC had found the C&NW–M&StL merger "clearly consistent with the public interest," further noting that "C&NW's proposal [was] 'the best for all concerned.'" Yet, not long after M&StL vanished into C&NW some shippers began to complain. During the 1960s and 1970s, C&NW rapidly pruned excess lines from its system. Most of the M&StL and CGW routes were truncated and abandoned piecemeal. In the end, little was left of the M&StL.

Continued on page 70.

Despite its bankruptcy, Penn Central's freight traffic remained robust. On April 10, 1971, a quartet of U25Bs lead more than a mile of piggyback trailers at Corfu, New York, on the former New York Central mainline. *Doug Eisele*

Opposite: Seaboard Coast Line's system map from its 1970 timetable. *Solomon collection*

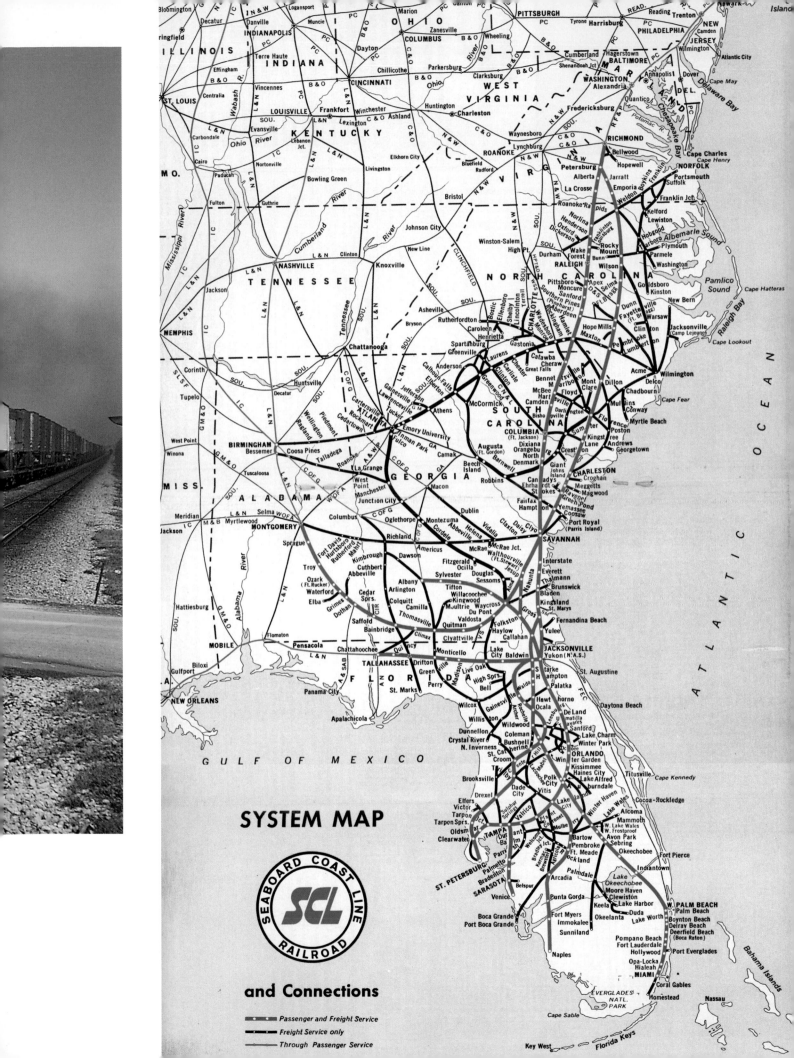

SYSTEM MAP

SEABOARD COAST LINE
SCL
RAILROAD

and Connections

Passenger and Freight Service

Freight Service only

Through Passenger Service

In April 1971, Seaboard Coast Line E-units and Penn Central's Metroliner rest side by side at Washington Terminal. In a month's time these railroads' passenger services would be absorbed by Amtrak, an operator specifically created by Congress to relieve ailing freight carriers from mounting passenger deficits. *George W. Kowanski*

Continued from page 67.

In the early 1980s, C&NW expanded into the Wyoming coal fields with Union Pacific's help. Meanwhile, it trimmed back many historic secondary routes and branches. Some were sold, many were abandoned. Finally, in 1995, UP absorbed what remained of C&NW, primarily for the coal lines and Omaha–Chicago corridor.

PENN CENTRAL'S EPIC FAIL

Penn Central was the big mama of railroad mergers. The union of Pennsylvania Railroad and New York Central not only represented the largest potential merger in terms of traffic, it precipitated countless merger proposals across the East. PRR-NYC merger talks were first announced in November 1957 then collapsed, only to resume again in 1961. PRR and NYC stockholders finally approved the union in May 1962. To overcome anticompetition objections, PRR divested its interest in Norfolk & Western and Wabash.

The ICC ultimately approved the PC merger but imposed several conditions, including the inclusion of New Haven Railroad, which had been bankrupt since 1961 and suffered from extraordinarily high passenger losses and severe highway competition. As another condition, PRR was compelled to sell its interest in Lehigh Valley to C&O or N&W, although neither wanted the beleaguered anthracite road. Penn Central began operations on February 1, 1968, and New Haven entered the fray on January 1, 1969.

Despite years of discussions, studies, and critical examination, Penn Central proved to be an ill-founded, poorly executed merger that exacerbated the component railroads' problems. Not only did it fail to cut costs, it actually accelerated the new railroad's desperate situation. By the end of 1968, Penn Central had a $2.8 million deficit that rose to $83 million by 1969. PC continued to hemorrhage money in 1970.

The problems with the railroad ran deep: a rigid and ossified rate structure, costly and obsolete labor agreements, extraordinary passenger deficits, a declining industrial base, years of inadequate and deferred maintenance, incompatible systems among component railroads, and managerial infighting and incompetence. The result was inevitable and catastrophic. On June 21, 1970, PC declared bankruptcy. It was the largest corporate bankruptcy in history up to that point. Many weak eastern railroads followed in PC's wake.

There was no simple way out of the mess and all of railroading would be changed by the time it was sorted out. One April 1, 1976, most of Penn Central's remaining operations were conveyed to Conrail. Exceptions included its Northeast Corridor (conveyed to Amtrak) and the Pittsburgh & Lake Erie, which took a separate route toward independence.

DREAM MERGER COMES TRUE WITH BURLINGTON NORTHERN

In 1956, more than 50 years after the breakup of Northern Securities had shaken the railroad world, Great Northern and Northern Pacific revived the long-coveted merger of the Hill empire. GN and NP controlled the Burlington lines and Spokane, Portland & Seattle, but this massive four-way union was contentious and controversial. Not everyone protested: Milwaukee Road thought it might benefit by demanding access to key points in the far West. After a decade of hearings and a succession of delays, the ICC approved the BN merger and the four lines became Burlington Northern on March 2, 1970. Fresh Cascade Green paint and a stylized "BN" became the face of the new railroad.

ILLINOIS CENTRAL GULF

Illinois Central and Gulf, Mobile & Ohio, mid-America's two major north-south railroads, were joined in August 1972, creating a system covering more than 9,630 miles and connecting Chicago with the Gulf of Mexico and significant secondary routes to various midwestern gateways, including Kansas City, Memphis, Omaha, and St. Louis. Duplication between the two systems led to draconian rationalization, and over the next two decades, more than two-thirds of ICG's route mileage was trimmed from the system map. IC's routes were largely favored over GM&O's.

Expansion and Contraction of Illinois Central System

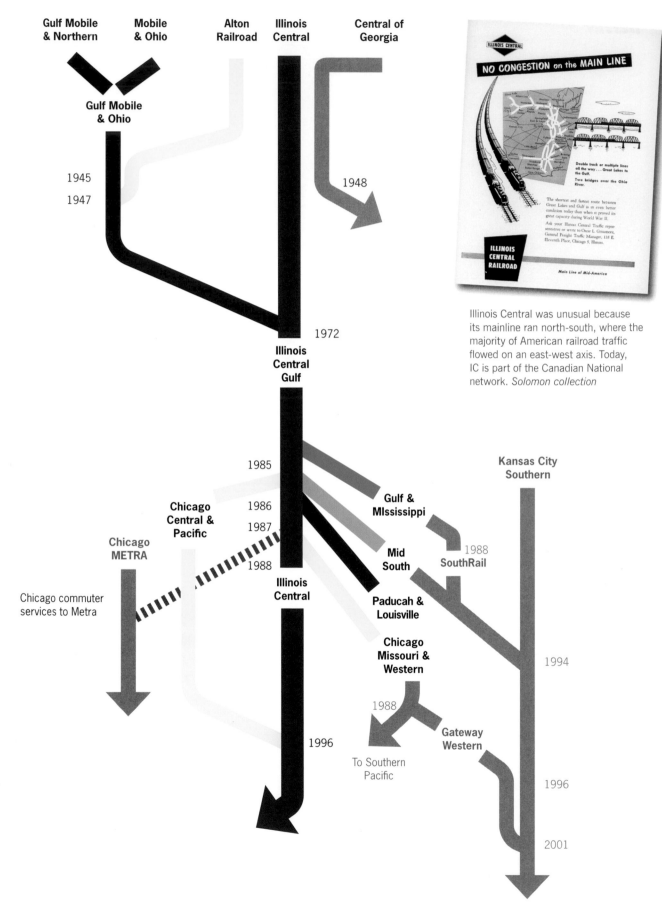

Gulf Mobile & Northern

Mobile & Ohio

Alton Railroad

Illinois Central

Central of Georgia

Gulf Mobile & Ohio

1945

1947

1948

NO CONGESTION on the MAIN LINE

ILLINOIS CENTRAL RAILROAD

Main Line of Mid-America

1972

Illinois Central Gulf

Illinois Central was unusual because its mainline ran north-south, where the majority of American railroad traffic flowed on an east-west axis. Today, IC is part of the Canadian National network. *Solomon collection*

1985

Kansas City Southern

Chicago Central & Pacific

1986

1987

Gulf & MIssissippi

Chicago METRA

1988

1988

SouthRail

Chicago commuter services to Metra

Mid South

Illinois Central

Paducah & Louisville

1994

Chicago Missouri & Western

1988

1996

Gateway Western

To Southern Pacific

1996

2001

During the 1980s, several significant regional railways were carved from the ICG empire. In 1988, the railroad, by then honed back to IC's north-south core, dropped "Gulf" and resumed its historic name.

CONRAIL MARKS FEDERAL ENTRY INTO RAILWAY BUSINESS

The collapse of Penn Central precipitated a series of railroad bankruptcies across the Northeast. Although some railroads, such as Central Railroad of New Jersey, were already bankrupt, by 1972 many major players from Maryland to Maine were in trouble. PC was viewed as beyond conventional reorganization, and the federal government stepped in to clean up the mess. In 1973, Congress passed the 3R Act, which put into motion the creation of the Consolidated Rail Corporation and established the United States Railway Association (not to be confused with the World War I–era USRA that operated the American network from 1917 to 1920), which in turn drafted plans and devised means for financing a government-created railroad to assume operations from the bankrupt companies.

The situation was complex and went beyond reorganizing the companies. Although the railroads were unprofitable, the service they provided remained crucial to the economy. Complicating matters were America's philosophical disagreements with the Soviet Union and Red China that made straightforward nationalization of railroad transport (which had also been accomplished by America's European allies) untenable to most parties involved. Although

Illinois Central Gulf blended operations of Illinois Central and Gulf, Mobile & Ohio. On June 24, 1979, a pair of ICG's Paducah Geeps (rebuilt at the Paducah, Kentucky, shops) leads a coal train on the former GM&O Alton Route at Joliet, Illinois. Santa Fe was parallel at this location, and a Santa Fe caboose can be seen at the end of an eastward train heading toward Chicago. *John Leopard*

Conrail was organized and financed in part by the federal government, the railroad was based on a private corporate model.

Planners found an excess railroad plant with too many routes, so Conrail was intended to pare back duplicate infrastructure while maintaining services and ultimately restoring sustainability. This was a tall order considering the corporate basket cases that were combined to form the new company.

On April 1, 1976, Conrail assumed most railway operations from Central Railroad of New Jersey, Erie Lackawanna, Lehigh & Hudson River, Lehigh Valley, Penn Central, Pennsylvania-Reading Seashore Lines, and Reading Company. From the time of creation, Conrail was less than the sum of its parts, but the USRA's Final System Plan was designed to weed out unsustainable, unnecessary, and redundant routes. In addition to marginal branches and secondary lines, Conrail saw the end of mainline operations on long sections of the Lehigh Valley and Erie Lackawanna.

With fresh blue and white paint covering the liveries of its component companies, Conrail initially struggled. Billions of federal dollars were infused into the operation. Finally, deregulation combined with improved management gave Conrail the tools it needed to return Northeast railroading to profitability.

Central Railroad of New Jersey had been affiliated with Reading Company since the nineteenth century and, as a result, was among railroads historically in B&O's sphere of influence. By the 1960s, it was suffering from declining freight traffic and extraordinarily high passenger deficits. CNJ declared bankruptcy in 1967 and in 1976 was among lines included in Conrail. A westbound CNJ freight passes Elizabeth, New Jersey, in April 1975. *George W. Kowanski*

Formation of Conrail

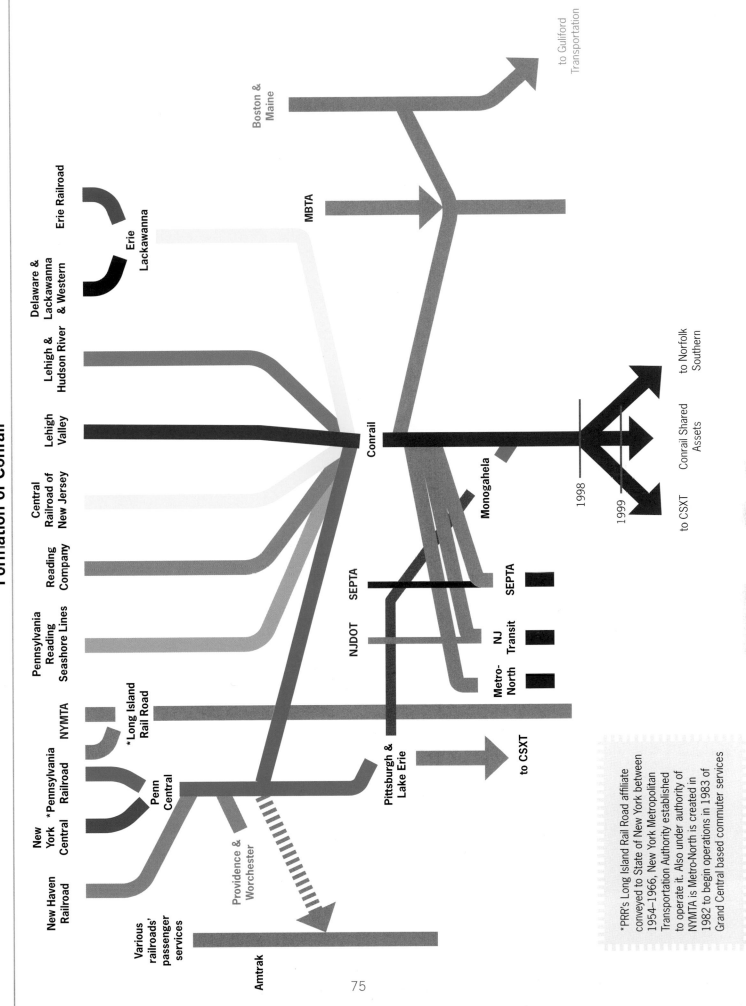

*PRR's Long Island Rail Road affiliate conveyed to State of New York between 1954–1966, New York Metropolitan Transportation Authority established to operate it. Also under authority of NYMTA is Metro-North is created in 1982 to begin operations in 1983 of Grand Central based commuter services

Among the goals of mergers in the 1960s and 1970s was elimination of duplicate and redundant plant. The derelict remains the Erie Railroad in western Indiana was part of Conrail's legacy. Had EL managed to remain out of Conrail, the Erie west end may have survived as a through mainline. *Brian Solomon*

Conrail was created by merging operations of a half-dozen bankrupt Northeastern railroads. Its early years were characterized by colorful fleets of decrepit locomotives inherited from predecessors. The railroad was only three weeks old when former Penn Central and Lehigh Valley Alco Centuries diesels were captured at Cleveland on May 21, 1976. *Bill Dechau, Doug Eisele Collection*

Chapter 4

EXTENDED FAMILIES

The Megamergers, 1980–2005

The mergers of the 1960s and 1970s focused on consolidation and retrenchment, while the megamerger movement that dawned in the 1980s was more about territorial expansion. In the 1980s and 1990s, railroad companies joined forces at a rapid rate that erased many historic names. By the year 2000, just seven super-sized freight railroads operated in the United States and Canada alongside a handful of big regionals and hundreds of short lines. The big railroads had focused traffic onto primary corridors leaving secondary routes to the small lines.

During this period, railroads enjoyed a renaissance spawned by deregulation. Traffic swelled and new technology changed the way railroads did business while greatly reducing the number of employees necessary to move trains. Not only did the railroads get bigger, in just about every respect the trains did, too. Railroading, which had suffered from decades of decline, was rejuvenated, yet many traditional lines were frozen out of new traffic as regulatory changes and consolidation effectively shut many small yards, deemphasized secondary routes, and routed traffic to the heaviest trunk lines. In the 1990s, traffic had grown to the point where the large railroads again suffered from congestion. Some routes, such as the former Northern Pacific crossing of Washington State's Stampede Pass and the old Erie Railroad mainline across western New York, saw renewed life. Where a decade earlier it appeared these lines might vanish entirely from the mainline map, they again functioned as through mainlines.

By virtue of their size, Burlington Northern in 1970 and Conrail in 1976 may be deemed the first of the "megamergers." Both railroads dwarfed traditional lines in terms of mileage and traffic. However, with the exception of Conrail, the mid- to late 1970s was a quiet time for serious railroad mergers. The underlying problems that resulted in the collapse of Penn Central and railroads across the East still hadn't been addressed, and merger was no longer viewed as the railroad cure-all. Worse, the rot that dragged eastern roads toward insolvency had spread to the Midwest.

Overleaf: Milwaukee Road was a "weak sister"; yet, its lines blanketed the upper Midwest and reached all the way to the Pacific Coast, fulfilling the "& Pacific" part of its name. But following the Burlington Northern merger of 1970, Milwaukee lost its ability to compete effectively. In November 1980—shortly before Milwaukee was reorganized, symbol freight 221 crossed the Mississippi River westbound at Sabula, Iowa. Today this old Milwaukee route is operated by Canadian Pacific subsidiary Iowa, Chicago & Eastern. *John Leopard*

Continued on page 86.

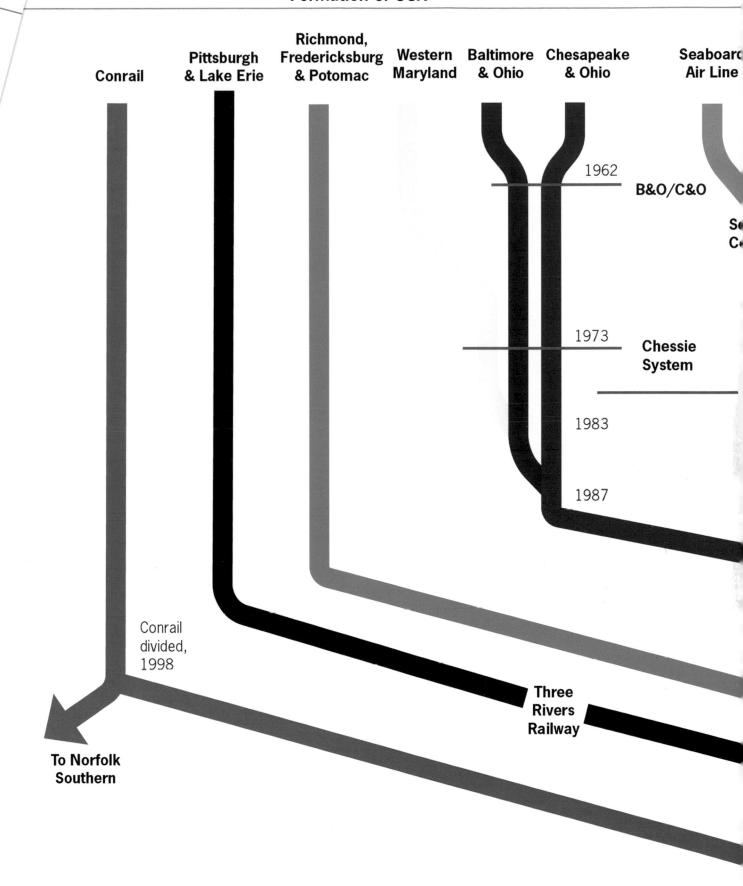

Conrail

Pittsburgh & Lake Erie

Richmond, Fredericksburg & Potomac

Western Maryland

Baltimore & Ohio

Chesapeake & Ohio

Seaboard Air Line

1962 — B&O/C&O

1973 — Chessie System

1983

1987

Conrail divided, 1998

To Norfolk Southern

Three Rivers Railway

Timeline

CSX	Kansas City Southern	Norfolk Southern	Union Pacific
71 Louisville & Nashville merger			
1973 Chessie System formed		1972 Erie Lackawanna bankrupt; DERECO dissolved	
April 1, 1976 Conrail begins operations; D&H granted extensive trackage rights		April 1, 1976 Conrail begins operations; D&H granted extensive trackage rights	
1979 Pittsburgh & Lake Erie independent		1979 Southern Railway conveys passenger service to Amtrak	
1980 CSX Corp. formed			1981 Western Pacific merges with Union Pacific
982 Western Maryland merged into Baltimore & Ohio		1982 NS formed from Norfolk & Western–Southern merger	1982 Missouri Pacific merges with UP and becomes a subsidiary company
983 Seaboard Systems formed			
1986 CSXT formed; Seaboard System absorbed			
1987 B&O merged into Chesapeake & Ohio and then C&O into CSXT			1988 Missouri-Kansas-Texas merges with UP's Missouri Pacific subsidiary
991 CSX acquires Richmond, Federicksburg & Potomac	1992 Kansas City Southern merges its Louisiana & Arkansas subsidiary		
1992 CSX acquires P&LE	1994 KCS buys Texas Mexican and Illinois Central spinoff MidSouth		1994 UP makes bid for ATSF
1996 CSX announces intent to y Conrail, sparking bidding war with Norfolk Southern	1996 KCS buys Gateway Western		1995 Chicago & North Western–UP merger
	1997 KCS negotiates role in NdeM spinoff TFM		1996 UP-SP merger
1997–1998 CSX and NS buy Conrail	1998 KCS buys 50 percent of Panama Railways	1997–1998 NS and CSX buy Conrail	
1999 CSX and NS divide Conrail operations		1999 NS and CSX divide Conrail operations	
	2005 TFM becomes KCS subsidiary	2005 NS and CP sign D&H traffic agreement	
		2007 NS and Pan Am Railways create Pan Am Southern joint venture	

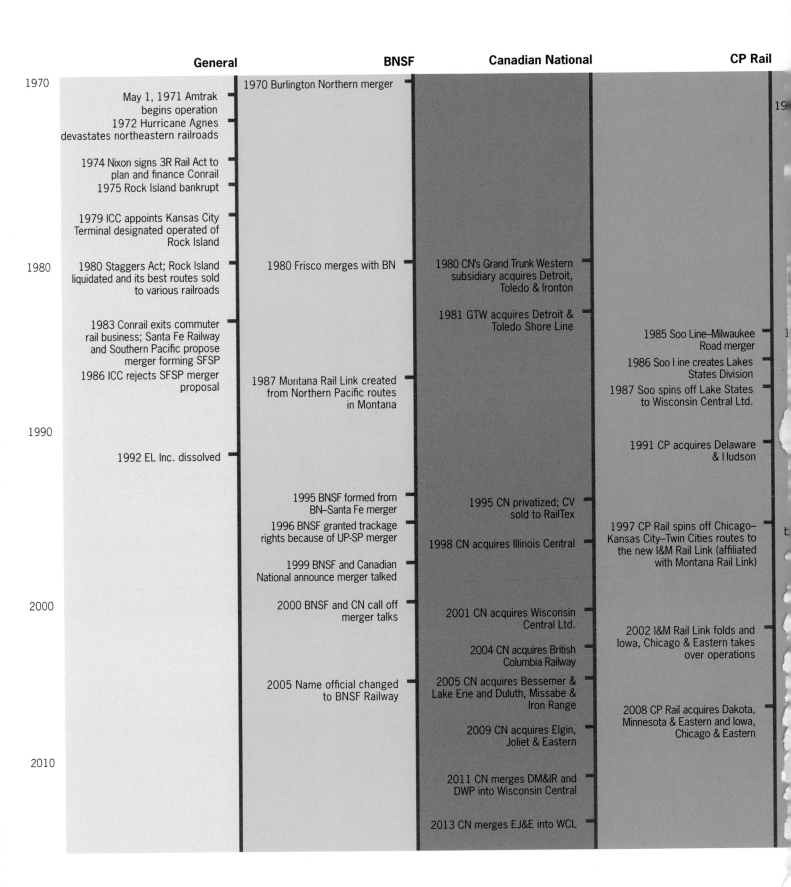

	General	BNSF	Canadian National	CP Rail
1970		1970 Burlington Northern merger		
	May 1, 1971 Amtrak begins operation			
	1972 Hurricane Agnes devastates northeastern railroads			
	1974 Nixon signs 3R Rail Act to plan and finance Conrail			
	1975 Rock Island bankrupt			
	1979 ICC appoints Kansas City Terminal designated operated of Rock Island			
1980	1980 Staggers Act; Rock Island liquidated and its best routes sold to various railroads	1980 Frisco merges with BN	1980 CN's Grand Trunk Western subsidiary acquires Detroit, Toledo & Ironton	
			1981 GTW acquires Detroit & Toledo Shore Line	
	1983 Conrail exits commuter rail business; Santa Fe Railway and Southern Pacific propose merger forming SFSP			1985 Soo Line–Milwaukee Road merger
				1986 Soo Line creates Lakes States Division
	1986 ICC rejects SFSP merger proposal	1987 Montana Rail Link created from Northern Pacific routes in Montana		1987 Soo spins off Lake States to Wisconsin Central Ltd.
1990				1991 CP acquires Delaware & Hudson
	1992 EL Inc. dissolved			
		1995 BNSF formed from BN–Santa Fe merger	1995 CN privatized; CV sold to RailTex	
		1996 BNSF granted trackage rights because of UP-SP merger		1997 CP Rail spins off Chicago–Kansas City–Twin Cities routes to the new I&M Rail Link (affiliated with Montana Rail Link)
			1998 CN acquires Illinois Central	
		1999 BNSF and Canadian National announce merger talked		
2000		2000 BNSF and CN call off merger talks	2001 CN acquires Wisconsin Central Ltd.	
				2002 I&M Rail Link folds and Iowa, Chicago & Eastern takes over operations
			2004 CN acquires British Columbia Railway	
		2005 Name official changed to BNSF Railway	2005 CN acquires Bessemer & Lake Erie and Duluth, Missabe & Iron Range	
				2008 CP Rail acquires Dakota, Minnesota & Eastern and Iowa, Chicago & Eastern
			2009 CN acquires Elgin, Joliet & Eastern	
2010			2011 CN merges DM&IR and DWP into Wisconsin Central	
			2013 CN merges EJ&E into WCL	

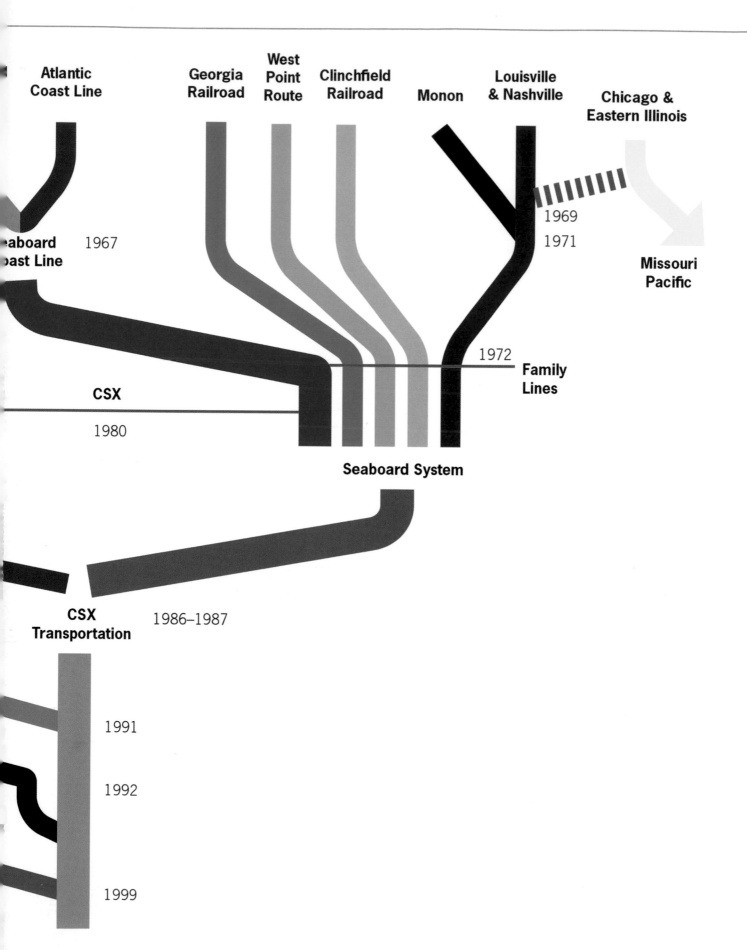

Atlantic
Coast Line

Georgia
Railroad

West
Point
Route

Clinchfield
Railroad

Monon

Louisville
& Nashville

Chicago &
Eastern Illinois

eaboard
oast Line

1967

1969

1971

Missouri
Pacific

1972

Family
Lines

CSX

1980

Seaboard System

CSX
Transportation

1986–1987

1991

1992

1999

Dawn of the megamerger era. When Burlington Northern bought Frisco in 1980, it precipitated an era of consolidation. By the time it was done, most of the old names in railroading had vanished into new corporate blends. On July 14, 1981, a pair of former Frisco SD45s with BN stencils rest at Northtown Yard, Minneapolis. *John Leopard*

Opposite: Conrail struggled in its early years as it blended a patchwork quilt of predecessors in an effort to make a profit from Northeastern railroading. On May 15, 1977, a potpourri of classic motive power works freight on Conrail's former Pennsylvania Railroad Main Line at South Fork, Pennsylvania. *George W. Kowanski*

Continued from page 78.

MAJOR MERGERS OF THE MIDWEST AND WEST

Rock Island, which had hoped to merge with Union Pacific in the 1960s, went to seed in the 1970s. By the time the ICC approved the merger of the two, UP was no longer interested and by 1975 Rock Island was bankrupt. The Rock had no future as a solvent company, and efforts to revitalize it failed. In 1980, it was liquidated with choice routes parceled out to other carriers.

Milwaukee Road was also in trouble. In the early 1980s, it reorganized, abandoning its Pacific Extension and paring down its Midwest network, selling off routes to short-line operators and Chicago's developing public suburban rail system (these latter routes emerging as Metra in the mid-1980s).

Two events kick-started the 1980s merger movement. First, federal deregulation of transportation—culminating with the Staggers Act of 1980—lifted many restrictions and relaxed government oversight of railroads and other modes while forcing railroads to seek the means to reduce costs in order to remain competitive. Second, Burlington Northern's acquisition of the St. Louis–San Francisco (the Frisco) and subsequent expansion into the South precipitated reaction throughout the industry.

There were other changes, too. In 1985, Canadian Pacific's Soo Line subsidiary absorbed the remains of Milwaukee Road. Less noticed was the Midwest expansion of Canadian

Continued on page 91

Union Pacific

Chicago & Eastern Illinois

Texas & Pacific

Missouri Pacific

Western Pacific

Union Pacific

Missouri-Kansas-Texas

Chicago & North Western

Minneapolis & St. Louis

Chicago Great Western

Southern Pacific

Cotton Belt

Denver & Rio Grande Western

Louisville & Nashville

C&EI operations divided between Missouri Pacific and Louisville & Nashville with eastern routes conveyed to L&N and western routes to MP. C&EI was then merged into the MP system.

Union Pacific

Missouri Pacific's image survived in first few years as part of the Union Pacific system; however, by the late 1980s, the name was phased out while UP reigned supreme. On May 3, 1985, a northward MP freight works Missouri-Kansas-Texas trackage at Hillsboro, Texas. M-K-T joined UP three years later. *John Leopard*

Buying a stairway to heaven: on March 15, 1980, Rock's sky-blue EMD diesels bumped along on rotten track. Rock ended operations two weeks later. Although it was liquidated, Rock's lines and equipment were sold off, which allowed many of its most important routes to survive into the modern era. *John Leopard*

Continued from page 86.

National's American subsidiary, Grand Trunk Western, which acquired the Detroit, Toledo & Ironton in 1980 and the Detroit & Toledo Shore Line a year later. Union Pacific added Missouri-Kansas-Texas to its empire in 1988.

In 1981–1982, Union Pacific had consummated a three-way merger with Western Pacific and Missouri Pacific. (While UP appeared the dominant partner, some observers noted that Missouri Pacific emerged as the force behind the expanded railroad.) Santa Fe Railway and Southern Pacific planned merger in 1983. Anticipating regulatory approval, the two combined their holding companies and even began painting locomotives in a new corporate livery only to have their case denied in 1986. (Diesels in SFSP paint served for another decade).

CONSOLIDATING THE EAST

In the East, holding companies for Norfolk & Western and Southern Railway merged in 1982, forming Norfolk Southern, and CSX Corporation was formed in 1980, joining the Chessie System and Seaboard Coast Line holding companies in anticipation of merger. CSX moved cautiously (see pages 84–85). In 1983, it consolidated the Family Lines railroads (Seaboard Coast Line, Louisville & Nashville, and affiliates) into the aptly named Seaboard System. Then, in 1986 and 1987, it merged Chessie and Seaboard System operations into the newly created CSX Transportation, which became the railroad's unified public image.

Continued on page 95.

Although in 1980, holding companies Chessie System and Seaboard Coast Line Industries merged to form CSX, this remained a latent force in railroad operations until the mid-1980s when it created CSX Transportation to absorb and operate component railroads. On a cloudless October 1993 day, a CSX SD40-2 on the old B&O approaches Altamont, Maryland. *Brian Solomon*

Previous: The 1970s-era Family Lines image was a branding of Louisville & Nashville and Seaboard Coast Line railroads. In 1983, this name was replaced by the short-lived Seaboard System before the railroads were blended into CSXT. On May 7, 1980, a southward L&N freight works the former Chicago & Eastern Illinois line at Watseka, Illinois. *George W. Kowanski*

In the 1980s, Guilford Transportation Industries mopped up Maine Central and Boston & Maine and briefly operated Delaware & Hudson. This consolidation initially focused traffic on B&M's east-west mainline via East Deerfield Yard (near Greenfield, Massachusetts). Then, in the early 1990s, GTI diverted most through traffic to Conrail at Worcester, Massachusetts, but the B&M line was revived following the Conrail split in 1999. Sunrise greets an eastward freight at East Deerfield on March 4, 2007. Today this route is operated as Pan Am Southern's Patriot Corridor—a joint venture between Pan Am Railways and Norfolk Southern. *Brian Solomon*

A pair of Canadian Pacific SD40-2s cross the Delaware & Hudson's Mohawk River bridge at Cohoes, New York. CP's American and Canadian Flag herald makes for an iconographic reflection of its expansion into the United States in the 1980s and 1990s. *Brian Solomon*

Delaware & Hudson Transitions

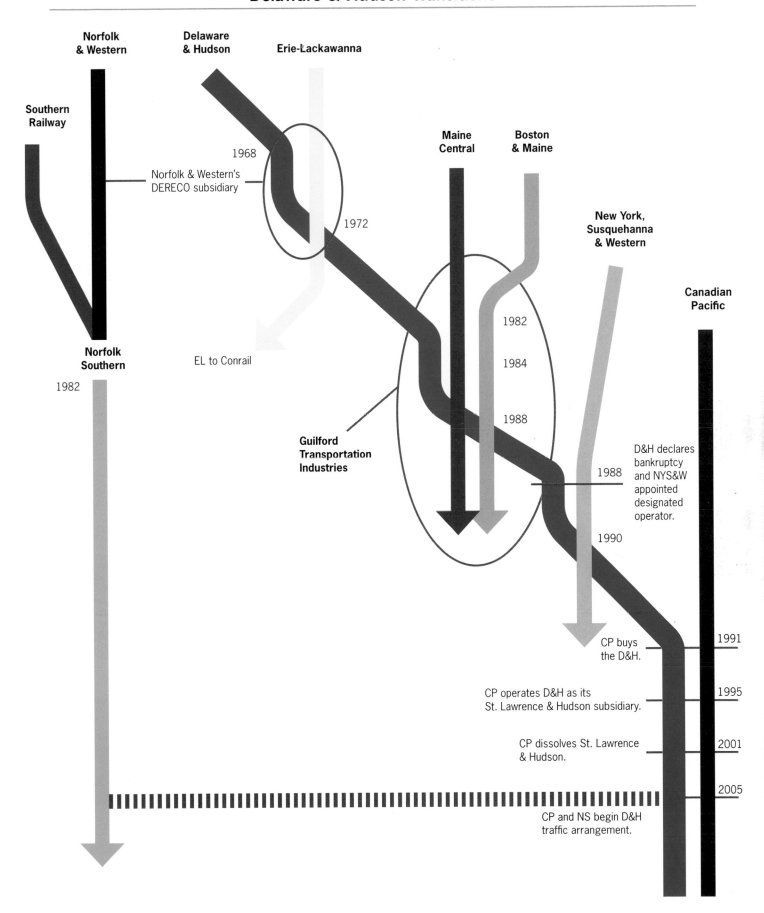

Southern Railway

Norfolk & Western

Delaware & Hudson

Erie-Lackawanna

1968

Norfolk & Western's DERECO subsidiary

1972

Maine Central

Boston & Maine

New York, Susquehanna & Western

Canadian Pacific

Norfolk Southern

EL to Conrail

1982

1982

1984

1988

Guilford Transportation Industries

D&H declares bankruptcy and NYS&W appointed designated operator.

1988

1990

CP buys the D&H.

1991

CP operates D&H as its St. Lawrence & Hudson subsidiary.

1995

CP dissolves St. Lawrence & Hudson.

2001

2005

CP and NS begin D&H traffic arrangement.

Southern Pacific maintained the identity of its Cotton Belt subsidiary until the 1990s. On November 24, 1986, Cotton Belt GP30 5002 leads the Owensville–St. Louis local freight on former Rock Island trackage east of Beaufort, Missouri. *Scott Muskopf*

Western Pacific survived attempted mergers with Southern Pacific and Santa Fe in the 1960s, but at the end of 1981, it faded into Union Pacific. While WP's routes remain largely intact, since the UP–SP merger of 1996, UP has gradually shifted traffic to parallel SP lines. *Brian Solomon*

Continued from page 91.

In the Northeast, Timothy Mellon assembled a network of railroads under the Guilford Transportation banner, beginning with the Maine Central in 1980 and followed by Boston & Maine in 1982 and Delaware & Hudson in 1984. Guilford's operation of the D&H was short-lived, however. In 1988, the line declared bankruptcy, and after a period of operation by the New York, Susquehanna & Western, D&H was bought by Canadian Pacific as part of CP's expanding American empire.

Conrail nearly floundered in its early years. It was initially kept afloat by an injection of federal funds that were used in part to buy new equipment and rebuild track. In the 1980s, deregulation, expert management, and harsh network and labor reductions finally made Conrail profitable. (Route mileage was trimmed from 17,000 in 1976 to 13,400 by 1984; employment was cut from 95,700 to approximately 39,000.) In the mid-1980s, Norfolk Southern expressed interest in merging with Conrail, but the timing wasn't right. Instead, Conrail was returned to the private sector in 1987 with a massive stock offering and flourished on its own for another decade before it was finally dissected by merger.

Following the rejection of the SFSP merger, the participating railroads took a few years to regroup. Southern Pacific and Rio Grande were unified by common ownership in 1988 (including SP's longtime affiliate, Cotton Belt). In 1990, SP expanded to Chicago.

As the big players vied for control of the most lucrative trunk routes, a side effect of deregulation was the creation of spinoff operations. Conrail began trimming its network with sales of line clusters to both new and existing short lines. These were organized to feed traffic to Conrail while minimizing interchange with competing railroads. In the mid-1980s, railroads began selling off large, marginally profitable routes, resulting in new but fairly large regional railroads, many of which were equivalent in route mileage to pre-1960s merger lines. CSX sold the former Buffalo, Rochester & Pittsburgh routes to Genesee & Wyoming, which created Rochester & Southern in 1986 and Buffalo & Pittsburgh in 1988. G&W grew into one of the largest short-line conglomerates. By 2013, it boasted more than 110 properties around the world.

MASSIVE MODERN SYSTEMS

In 1994, Burlington Northern and Santa Fe shook the industry with their unpredicted proposed merger. Union Pacific responded by making a controversial counter offer for Santa Fe, which was rebuffed. BNSF was approved by the ICC and began operations in September 1995, by which time Union Pacific had merged with its longtime traffic partner, Chicago & North Western. Union Pacific next moved to acquire the Southern Pacific/Rio Grande empire. As this massive undertaking was unfolding, the ICC was disbanded and its regulatory and merger functions allocated to the newly created Surface Transportation Board. The STB approved UP-SP, and the union was consummated in 1996. The UP-SP combination was so big, and the two networks overlapped in so many areas, that to maintain competition STB authorized extensive trackage rights to competitors, chiefly BNSF and KCS (primarily in Texas). The result was largely a two-railroad network across most of the far West. It was as if Hill and Harriman had partitioned railroading in their afterlife.

While two neatly overlapping systems dominated the West, the East was complicated by three major systems and growing competition from the major Canadian networks and several key regional players. Especially complicated was the dominant role played by Conrail, which, by virtue of its creation, had a near monopoly in much of the Northeast. The situation made a conventional merger between Conrail and any other major player difficult since enlargement would only further freeze out competition. In the mid-1990s, NS re-explored merger with Conrail only to be trumped by a CSX merger bid in 1996. A contest between the two eastern giants ensued. Ultimately CSX and NS agreed to divide Conrail and jointly acquired the property during in 1997 and 1998. Operations were split in spring 1999, while Conrail's "Joint Assets" continued to serve both carriers in complex terminal areas such as New Jersey and Detroit where it was impossible to satisfactorily separate infrastructure. With Conrail divided, most major eastern markets were served by both NS and CSX or by their connections.

Kansas City Southern is among the last traditional names in railroading. By the mid-1990s, it was faced with being absorbed by one of the growing mega systems or expanding on its own. It chose the latter and began a series of strategic acquisitions in 1994 with the purchase of the Texas Mexican and Illinois Central Gulf spinoff, MidSouth. Where most American mergers have focused on east-west markets, KCS had developed a north-south network aimed at fostering traffic with Mexico. Key to KCS's expansion was involvement with the newly created National Railways of Mexico privatized franchise, Transportación Ferroviaria Mexicana, in 1997. KCS later increased its involvement with TFM, which in 2005 became KCS subsidiary Kansas City Southern de Mexico. KCS also partnered with NS in developing the east-west Meridian Corridor, based on the old MidSouth route, as a southern transcontinental route.

One traditional line that sat out the waves of merger mania was Florida East Coast. Although FEC was acquired by Fortress in 2007, which later controlled the RailAmerica short-line group, it has not been merged into any of the larger systems as of 2013.

Kansas City Southern Expansion

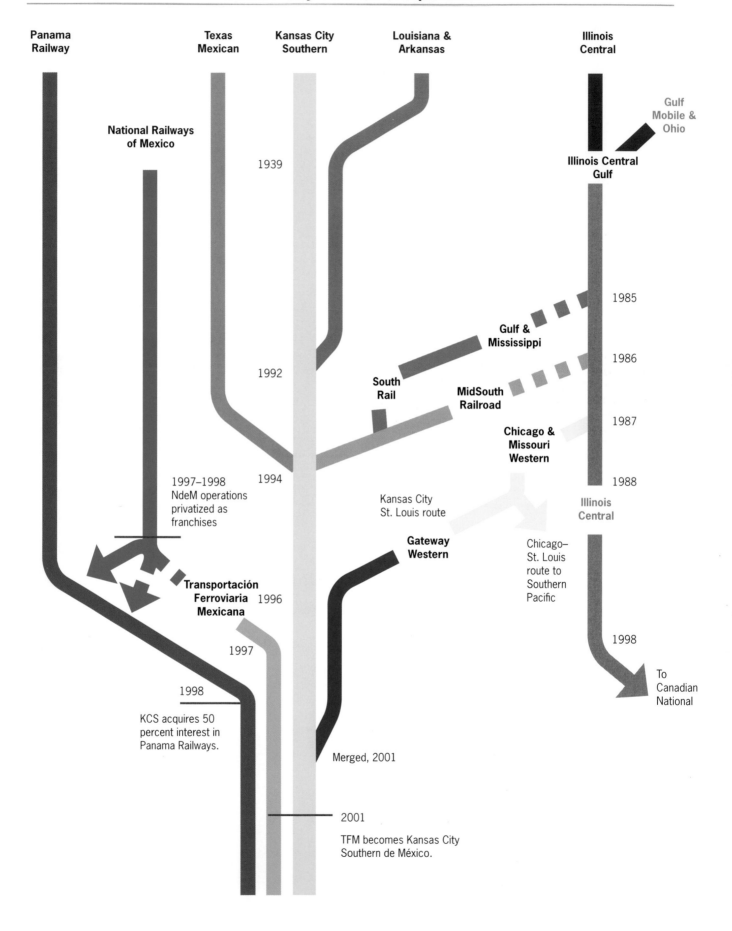

Panama Railway

Texas Mexican

Kansas City Southern

Louisiana & Arkansas

Illinois Central

National Railways of Mexico

1939

Gulf Mobile & Ohio

Illinois Central Gulf

1985

Gulf & Mississippi

1986

1992

South Rail

MidSouth Railroad

1987

Chicago & Missouri Western

1988

1997–1998 NdeM operations privatized as franchises

1994

Kansas City St. Louis route

Illinois Central

Transportación Ferroviaria Mexicana

1996

Gateway Western

Chicago–St. Louis route to Southern Pacific

1997

1998

KCS acquires 50 percent interest in Panama Railways.

1998

To Canadian National

Merged, 2001

2001

TFM becomes Kansas City Southern de México.

CANADIAN CONQUESTS

The Canadian railroads also underwent substantial transformation during the megamerger period. Both Canadian National and Canadian Pacific already operated Canadian transcontinental systems. However, as events in the United States transpired, both pared back their domestic operations, especially in weak traffic areas such as the Maritime provinces while making notable expansions into the United States. CP's Soo Line merged with Milwaukee Road in 1985; in 1986, Soo created its Lakes States Transportation Division from its old Soo Line/Wisconsin Central routes east of the Twin Cities to Chicago (see page 103). In 1987, this division was spun off and became the core of Wisconsin Central Limited's regional empire. (While WCL operated the historic Wisconsin Central route, no corporate connection existed between the railroads.) In 1990, CP further expanded its U.S. empire by acquiring Delaware & Hudson. (After D&H's 1988 bankruptcy, it had been temporarily operated by New York, Susquehanna & Western under court directive.)

In 1995, CN was privatized, and while it sold off its Central Vermont Railway affiliate that year, it made a series of U.S. acquisitions beginning with the Illinois Central in 1998. CN and BNSF discussed merger in 1999, but STB's unfavorable stance discouraged further talks and the railroads broke off plans in 2000. In 2001, CN picked up Wisconsin Central Limited (an ironic twist, considering WCL had largely been a CP/Soo Line property) and went on to add the former US Steel roads to its portfolio, albeit at different times. CN also expanded in western Canada, picking up British Columbia Railway in 2004.

In the mid-1990s, CP spun off Soo Line's former Milwaukee Road route between Chicago and Kansas City (including feeders and a connection from Sabula, Iowa, to the Twin Cities). A decade later it brought these routes back into the fold, along with regional Dakota, Minnesota & Eastern (which controlled the former CP lines as its Iowa, Chicago & Eastern affiliate) as part of a move aimed at gaining access to Powder River coal traffic. CP also partnered with Norfolk Southern in regards to traffic moving on its Delaware & Hudson routes, some of which now see more of NS's through trains than CP's.

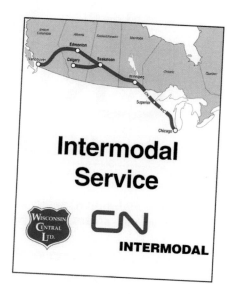

In 1996, Wisconsin Central Limited and Canadian National announced an intermodal connection via Superior, Wisconsin. Five years later CN absorbed WCL into its expanding network in the United States. *Solomon collection*

Chapter 5

FAMILY TRAVEL

**Passenger Railroad Transitions to Public Ownership,
1960–1995**

NATIONALIZED PASSENGER RAILS

Despite massive investment in modern equipment after World War II, American passenger railroading fell into a financial tailspin. While the passenger business had long been the smaller share of railroad revenue, changes to cost structures, declining ridership, and enormous government subsidies to competing modes took their toll. By the late 1950s, unsubsidized passenger railroading was no longer sustainable. Railroads that had been chipping away at their passenger schedules began to cut their passenger networks in earnest following the Transportation Act of 1958, which eased their ability to discontinue services. The death knell for many famous name trains came when the U.S. Post Office opted not to renew most railroad mail contracts in 1967. Mail had historically offered a staple source of revenue for intercity passenger services and had been integral to their operations and business model.

The onset of the Penn Central bankruptcy and eastern railroad insolvency forced government action. Facing rising operating losses, eastern railroads were desperate for relief, and easing passenger train deficits was viewed as part of a solution. In 1970 and 1971, Congress created the National Railroad Passenger Corporation, better known by the trade name Amtrak "to provide financial assistance for and establishment of a national rail passenger system, to provide for the modernization of railroad passenger equipment, to authorize the prescribing of minimum standards for railroad passenger service." Amtrak facilitated the continuation of passenger services while shifting the financial burden from the private railroads to federal and

Penn Central was by far the largest passenger carrier in the United States; its financial woes spurred the creation of Amtrak and encouraged increased public responsibility for suburban rail operations across the Northeast region. In April 1970, a Penn Central GG1 electric leads the New York-Florida *Champion* at North Philadelphia. *George W. Kowanski*

Amtrak assumed operation of most long distance American passenger trains on May 1, 1971. In its early years, Amtrak assigned hand-me-down equipment to most of its trains, while it neither owned track nor supplied its own operating crews. On September 28, 1976, Amtrak train 73 rolling through the Mohawk River Valley on the former New York Central passes Palentine Bridge, New York. *George W. Kowanski*

state governments. Railroads had the option of joining and providing Amtrak with cash or equipment, or opting out and continuing to provide their own intercity passenger services out of pocket. Excluded from Amtrak were short-distance suburban services.

Seventeen railroads signed contracts with Amtrak in 1971. Rio Grande, Rock Island, and Southern Railway were among the lines that continued to run their own trains. However, Southern joined in 1979 and Rio Grande in 1983, while Rock Island went the way of the dodo bird with its surviving suburban trains becoming the domain of Chicago's Regional Transportation Authority.

Initially, Amtrak neither owned railway lines nor employed its own operating crews. It acquired most of the Northeast Corridor (Boston to Washington, D.C.) from Penn Central in 1976. Amtrak assumed operational responsibility for its trains in the 1980s and began using its own crews. Today ownership and control of Amtrak routes varies from route to route; while it controls most of the Northeast Corridor and key portions of the Empire and Keystone corridors, as well as portions of other lines, Amtrak mostly serves lines owned and operated by private freight railroads.

Long-Distance Passenger Services Conveyed to AMTRAK

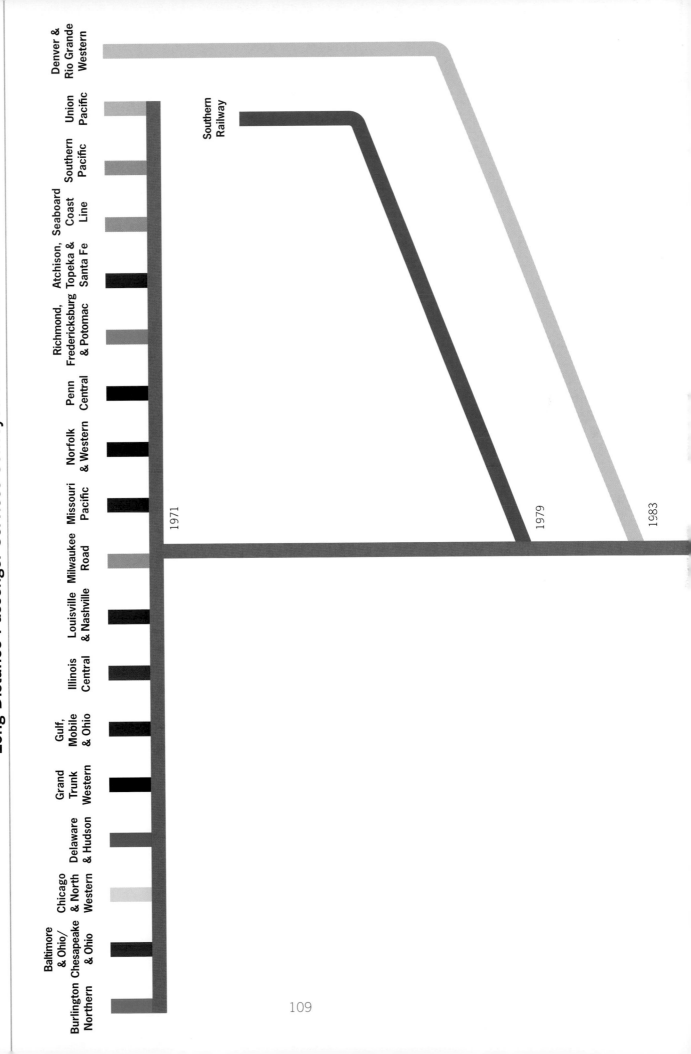

Denver & Rio Grande Western

Union Pacific

Southern Railway

Southern Pacific

Atchison, Topeka & Santa Fe

Seaboard Coast Line

Richmond, Fredericksburg & Potomac

Penn Central

Norfolk & Western

Missouri Pacific

Milwaukee Road

Louisville & Nashville

Illinois Central

Gulf, Mobile & Ohio

Grand Trunk Western

Delaware & Hudson

Chicago & North Western

Baltimore & Ohio/ Chesapeake & Ohio

Burlington Northern

1971

1979

1983

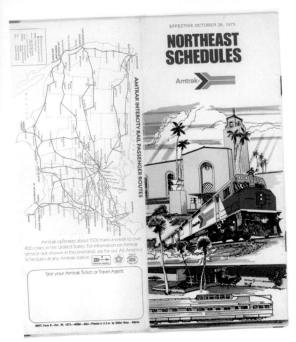

Amtrak's October 26, 1975, public Northeast schedules feature an artist depiction of an EMD-built SDP40F, Los Angeles's Union Passenger Station, and one of Amtrak's more modern "Amshacks," along with a classic Budd-built dome observation car. *Solomon collection*

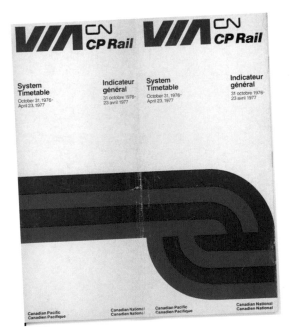

Like Amtrak, VIA Rail was a 1970s creation. This timetable, taking effect October 31, 1976, and showing both Canadian National and Canadian Pacific routes, is one of VIA's earliest public documents. *Solomon collection*

Opposite: VIA Rail is Canada's equivalent to Amtrak, the national intercity passenger service provider. It began operations in the late 1970s and largely serves Canadian National and Canadian Pacific routes. A westward VIA train departs Toronto with the CN tower looming above like an alien landing beacon. *Brian Solomon*

VIA RAIL CANADA

VIA Rail is Canada's equivalent of Amtrak, providing a nationwide intercity passenger rail network on Canadian National and Canadian Pacific routes. VIA's creation was less complex than Amtrak's since it involved only two primary operators; the largest of which, CN, was already a nationalized railroad. VIA began in 1976 as a CN marketing name. It was incorporated in 1978 and assumed most functions of CN and CP intercity passenger services.

Suburban Rails

Historically, commuter rail operations were the domain of private railroads. In the days when railroads viewed passenger trains as profitable ventures, commuter service seemed an ideal revenue source. Commuter travel patterns were predictable (morning inbound, evening outbound) and reliable (most passengers used the services five days a week). Furthermore, suburban passengers didn't require complicated baggage facilities or specialized rolling stock.

From the mid-nineteenth century, key railroads embraced commuter operations. America's earliest suburbs were railroad-based towns along lines radiating from Boston. Later, railroad suburbs emerged around New York City, Philadelphia, and Chicago. San Francisco enjoyed a highly developed suburban heavy-rail service (and also featured extensive heavy interurban electric lines run by Southern Pacific subsidiaries and other companies).

Between 1900 and the early 1930s, several railroads made significant investments to expand and improve suburban operations. This often included electrification and modern, steel-body cars. Pennsylvania Railroad electrified its Long Island Rail Road subsidiary's lines with third rail then added high-voltage overhead to its Philadelphia services. (Ultimately PRR extended wires to its New York–Washington, D.C., mainlines, North Jersey suburban lines, numerous freight cutoffs, and from Philadelphia west to Harrisburg.) New York Central adopted third rail for its Grand Central–based passenger services. New Haven Railroad used NYC's third rail to access Grand Central but wired its services east to its Connecticut namesake, along with branches to Danbury and New Canaan, Connecticut. (New Haven's system, like PRR's, began with suburban operations but soon moved to most aspects of its urban passenger and freight operations.) Philadelphia enjoyed some of the most extensive suburban services, with Reading Company's electrified competing with PRR's (in some places, lines were side by side). Chicago enjoyed suburban services radiating in every direction. Most intensive were Illinois Central's services south from downtown

Penn Central FL9s pass Stamford, Connecticut, on April 5, 1972. Since January 1983, Metro-North has operated former New Haven Railroad commuter services based at Grand Central Terminal. What was a privately operated unified freight and passenger railroad under New Haven (until 1969) is now operated by no less than a dozen railroads and public agencies. *Walter E. Zullig Jr.*

that were electrified in the 1920s. But not all of Chicago's railroads hosted intense commuter services—Santa Fe, Chicago Great Western, and Soo Line were among the lines that didn't embrace highly developed commuter traffic.

After World War I, higher wage scales, rising fuel costs, and growing automobile ownership gradually eroded suburban service profitability. After World War II many suburban services were losing money, and during the 1950s and 1960s the problem grew acute. While railroads lost the ability to make a profit carrying commuters, cities recognized that suburban services were an important part of the urban fabric. To maintain these services, cities needed to break the taboo of public support for private railroads and find ways to fund money-losing services without causing an ideological uproar. The transitions took different paths in each major city and were introduced in stages over a number of years.

Eastern railroads, already suffering from economic woes, were the first to benefit from public relief as communities, and the federal government began to provide economic assistance in the form of operating subsidies and funds to renew equipment and stations. Ultimately, communities took ownership of key railway lines and became responsible for train operations.

PUBLIC OWNERSHIP OF LONG ISLAND RAIL ROAD

As a subsidiary of the Pennsylvania Railroad, Long Island Rail Road had benefited from extensive electrification. It offered the most intensive suburban service in the United States, reaching from the eastern tip of Long Island to New York City terminals, including Penn Station in Manhattan.

Northeast Commuter Lines

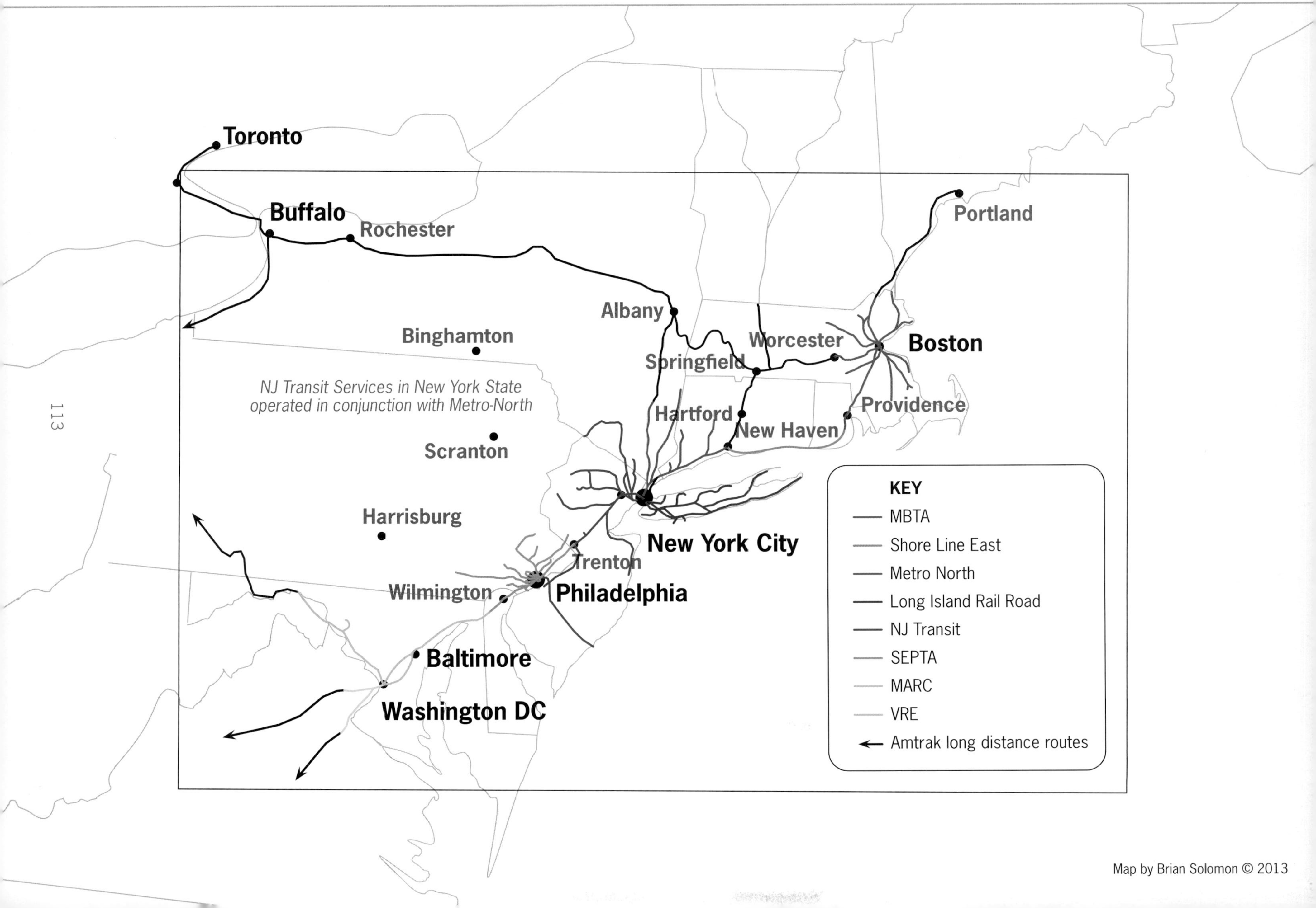

Toronto
Buffalo
Rochester
Albany
Binghamton
NJ Transit Services in New York State operated in conjunction with Metro-North
Scranton
Harrisburg
Springfield
Worcester
Boston
Portland
Hartford
New Haven
Providence
New York City
Trenton
Philadelphia
Wilmington
Baltimore
Washington DC
KEY
MBTA
Shore Line East
Metro North
Long Island Rail Road
NJ Transit
SEPTA
MARC
VRE
Amtrak long distance routes

Map by Brian Solomon © 2013

Former New York Central commuter operations required more than a dozen years to make the transition from public to private operation. In this July 16, 1981, view FL9s lettered for Conrail and Penn Central lead a Grand Central–bound passenger train at Marble Hill, in the Bronx, New York. *Walter E. Zullig Jr.*

LIRR was unusual because of the exceptional density of its railway network and passenger traffic that vastly exceeded its freight service. However, by the late 1940s, PRR was unwilling to sustain further losses from LIRR, which declared bankruptcy in 1949. Rather than discontinuing services that sustained high ridership, PRR worked with New York state and New York City to allow public responsibility for LIRR's network. Public involvement began in 1954 and, over the years, made a series of transitions that resulted in full public ownership of LIRR in 1966.

New York state set up the Metropolitan Transportation Authority (MTA) to operate the railroad. Ultimately, the MTA became the umbrella organization overseeing operations of New York City's public transport services, including its subways and buses, as well as Grand Central–based suburban rail routes provided by Metro-North.

SEPTA COMES TO PHILLY

In 1958, Philadelphia began providing operating subsidies for Pennsylvania Railroad and Reading Company suburban services within the city limits. The arrangement was expanded to include service to suburban counties in 1964, a move facilitated by the creation of the South Eastern Pennsylvania Transportation Authority. While initially focused on PRR and Reading trains, SEPTA ultimately unified management of most Philadelphia-area public transportation, including subways, buses, trolleys, and the Norristown high-speed third-rail line (remnant of a former interurban electric line). Although commuter rail services were administered by SEPTA, host railroads continued to operate trains through the 1970s.

Continued on page 120.

For more than half a century, Pennsylvania Railroad's Tuscan-red, owl-eye, MP54 electric multiple units were a trademark of its Philadelphia suburban services. *Richard Jay Solomon*

115

Septa Timeline

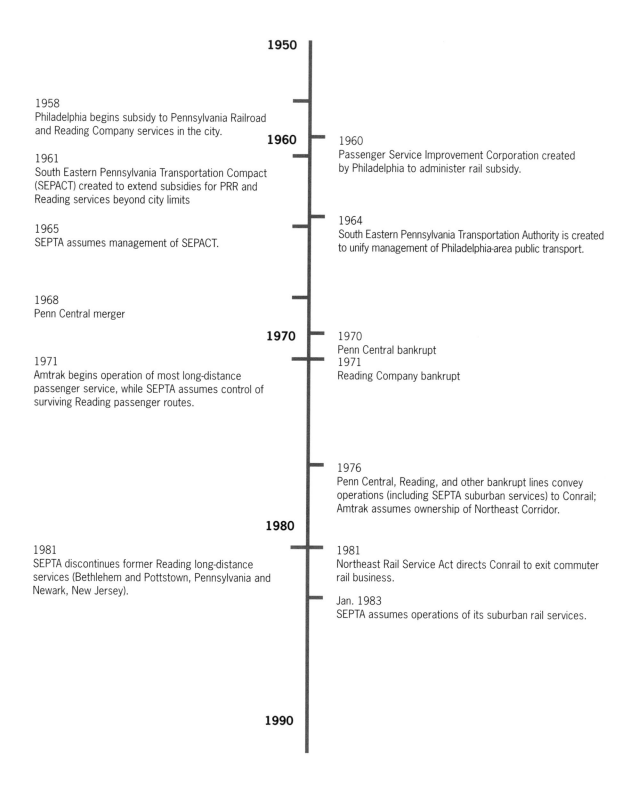

1950

1958
Philadelphia begins subsidy to Pennsylvania Railroad and Reading Company services in the city.

1960

1960
Passenger Service Improvement Corporation created by Philadelphia to administer rail subsidy.

1961
South Eastern Pennsylvania Transportation Compact (SEPACT) created to extend subsidies for PRR and Reading services beyond city limits

1964
South Eastern Pennsylvania Transportation Authority is created to unify management of Philadelphia-area public transport.

1965
SEPTA assumes management of SEPACT.

1968
Penn Central merger

1970

1970
Penn Central bankrupt
1971
Reading Company bankrupt

1971
Amtrak begins operation of most long-distance passenger service, while SEPTA assumes control of surviving Reading passenger routes.

1976
Penn Central, Reading, and other bankrupt lines convey operations (including SEPTA suburban services) to Conrail; Amtrak assumes ownership of Northeast Corridor.

1980

1981
SEPTA discontinues former Reading long-distance services (Bethlehem and Pottstown, Pennsylvania and Newark, New Jersey).

1981
Northeast Rail Service Act directs Conrail to exit commuter rail business.

Jan. 1983
SEPTA assumes operations of its suburban rail services.

1990

East Coast Commuter Services

Transition from Private to Public Operation

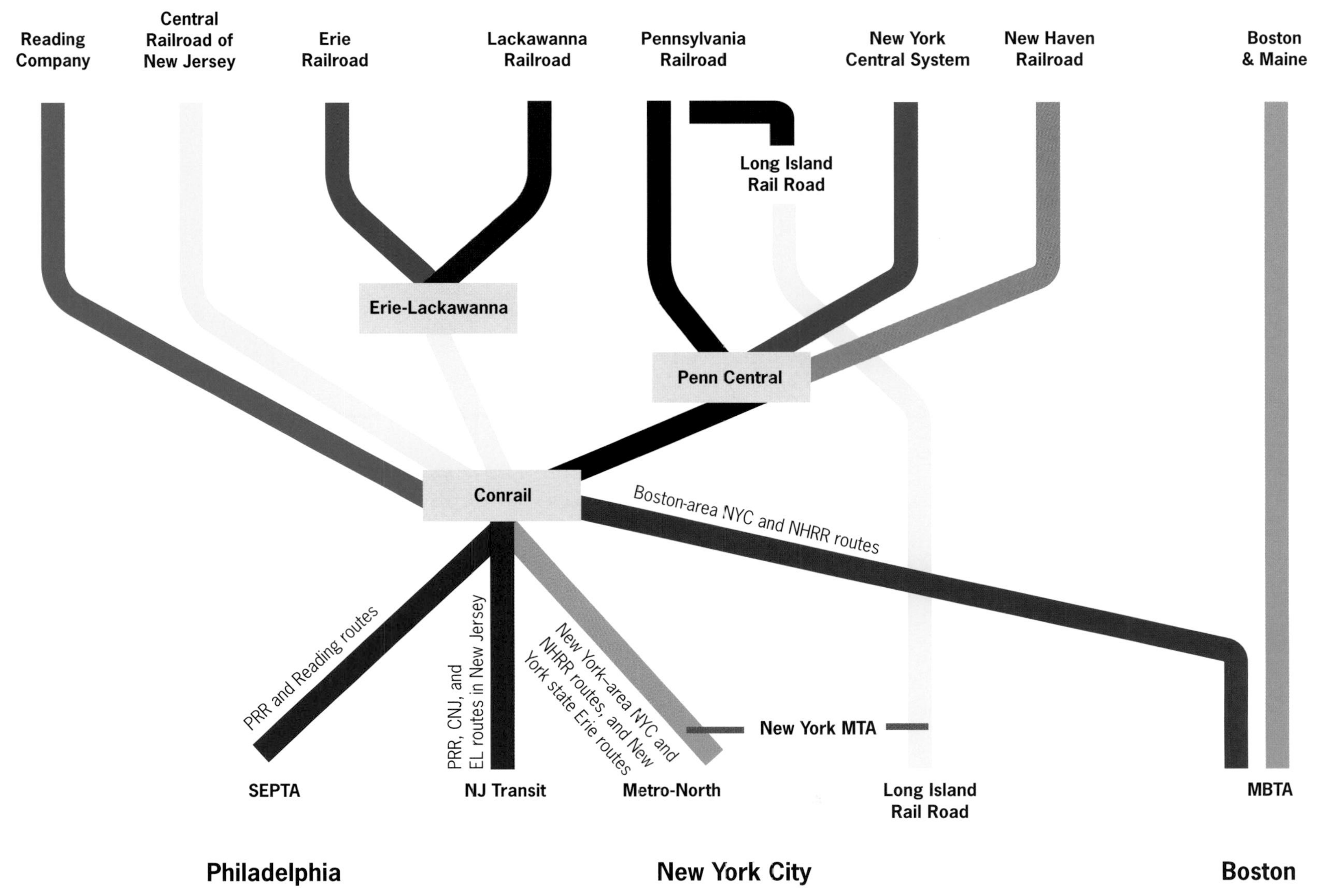

Reading Company

Central Railroad of New Jersey

Erie Railroad

Lackawanna Railroad

Pennsylvania Railroad

Long Island Rail Road

New York Central System

New Haven Railroad

Boston & Maine

Erie-Lackawanna

Penn Central

Conrail

Boston-area NYC and NHRR routes

New York–area NYC and NHRR routes, and New York state Erie routes

PRR, CNJ, and EL routes in New Jersey

PRR and Reading routes

New York MTA

Long Island Rail Road

Metro-North

NJ Transit

SEPTA

MBTA

Philadelphia

New York City

Boston

MBTA Timeline

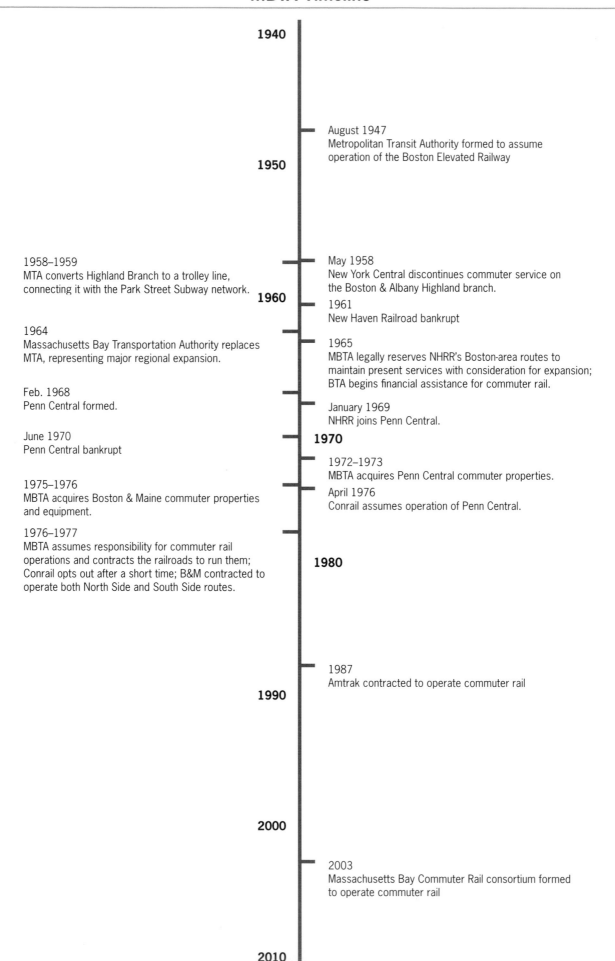

1940

1950

August 1947
Metropolitan Transit Authority formed to assume
operation of the Boston Elevated Railway

1958–1959
MTA converts Highland Branch to a trolley line,
connecting it with the Park Street Subway network.

May 1958
New York Central discontinues commuter service on
the Boston & Albany Highland branch.

1960

1961
New Haven Railroad bankrupt

1964
Massachusetts Bay Transportation Authority replaces
MTA, representing major regional expansion.

1965
MBTA legally reserves NHRR's Boston-area routes to
maintain present services with consideration for expansion;
BTA begins financial assistance for commuter rail.

Feb. 1968
Penn Central formed.

January 1969
NHRR joins Penn Central.

June 1970
Penn Central bankrupt

1970

1972–1973
MBTA acquires Penn Central commuter properties.

1975–1976
MBTA acquires Boston & Maine commuter properties
and equipment.

April 1976
Conrail assumes operation of Penn Central.

1976–1977
MBTA assumes responsibility for commuter rail
operations and contracts the railroads to run them;
Conrail opts out after a short time; B&M contracted to
operate both North Side and South Side routes.

1980

1987
Amtrak contracted to operate commuter rail

1990

2000

2003
Massachusetts Bay Commuter Rail consortium formed
to operate commuter rail

2010

NJ Transit Timeline

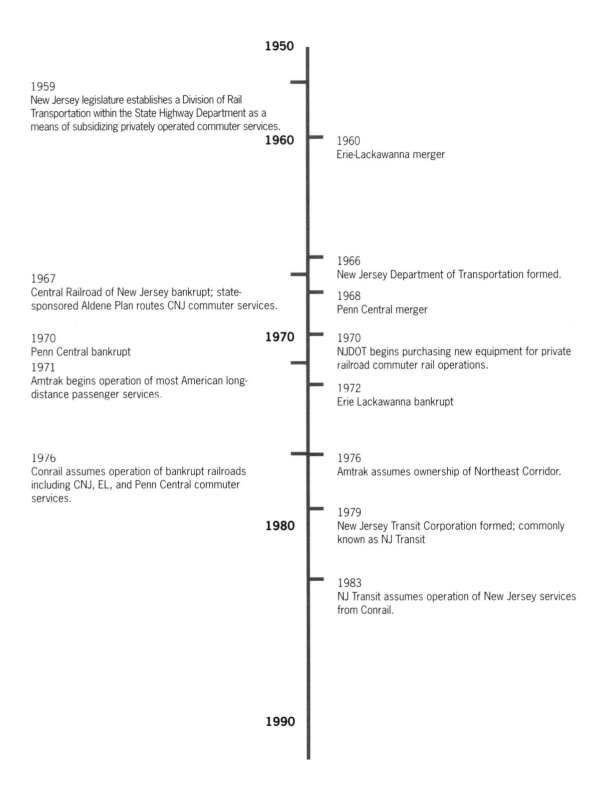

1950

1959
New Jersey legislature establishes a Division of Rail Transportation within the State Highway Department as a means of subsidizing privately operated commuter services.

1960

1960
Erie-Lackawanna merger

1966
New Jersey Department of Transportation formed.

1967
Central Railroad of New Jersey bankrupt; state-sponsored Aldene Plan routes CNJ commuter services.

1968
Penn Central merger

1970
Penn Central bankrupt

1970

1970
NJDOT begins purchasing new equipment for private railroad commuter rail operations.

1971
Amtrak begins operation of most American long-distance passenger services.

1972
Erie Lackawanna bankrupt

1976
Conrail assumes operation of bankrupt railroads including CNJ, EL, and Penn Central commuter services.

1976
Amtrak assumes ownership of Northeast Corridor.

1979
New Jersey Transit Corporation formed; commonly known as NJ Transit

1980

1983
NJ Transit assumes operation of New Jersey services from Conrail.

1990

Continued from page 115.

Opposite: In January 2013, a SEPTA Silverliner V approaches the former Reading Company station at Norristown, Pennsylvania, as a 100-route high-speed car rests between runs on the elevated former Philadelphia & Western line overhead. SEPTA offers a well-integrated intermodal transit system in the greater Philadelphia area. *Brian Solomon*

In addition to operating subsidies, SEPTA made possible a variety of infrastructure improvements, including electrification of Reading's lines to Fox Chase in 1966 and to Warminster in 1974, as well as the planning of the Center City Commuter Tunnel that linked PRR and Reading electric suburban routes in the 1980s.

Conrail assumed operation of Philadelphia-based service in 1976 (although in the Conrail era trains were lettered either for predecessors or SEPTA). The Northeast Rail Act of 1981 mandated that Conrail exit the commuter rail business at the end of 1982, and in January 1983, SEPTA became its own train operator. Although the early years of SEPTA operation were characterized by rundown equipment and curtailed services as result of decaying infrastructure and other inherited problems, today Philadelphia enjoys one of best integrated public transit system in the United States.

WICKED GOOD COMMUTER SERVICE ON THE MBTA

In 1947, Boston's Metropolitan Transit Authority (abbreviated MTA, not to be confused with New York City's similarly named agency) was created to assume operations of the financially ailing Boston Elevated Railway (provider of streetcar and rapid-transit services). MTA was replaced in 1964 with an expanded agency called Massachusetts Bay Transportation Authority, aimed at aiding heavy-rail suburban services and other public transportation serving greater Boston. MBTA is similar to Philadelphia's SEPTA, providing multimodal public transport across the metropolitan area, including interstate suburban rail services, but is strictly a regional operation that doesn't span the entire state. In Boston, MBTA is known colloquially as "The T" and is an integral part of the city's infrastructure.

Boston was among the first proactive cities in converting private heavy-rail services to public operation. In the late 1950s, it acquired New York Central's Boston & Albany Highland Branch and, in 1960, transformed it into a rapid-transit extension of the Park Street Subway using PCC trolley cars. In 1965, MBTA began providing financial subsidy to commuter services and secured New Haven Railroad routes serving Boston for use as commuter lines. This was part of a greater strategy to preserve railways serving Boston as all three of Boston's major railroads descended into bankruptcy: New Haven in 1961, and Boston & Maine and Penn Central (New Haven's and New York Central's successor) in 1970.

Overleaf: An outbound MBTA train for Worcester, Massachusetts, runs west along the Mass-Turnpike at Newtonville, Massachusetts. To make room for the Mass-Turnpike extension to Boston, in the early 1960s, New York Central sacrificed two of its four tracks on the Boston & Albany mainline between Riverside, Massachusetts, and South Station. *Brian Solomon*

During 1972 and 1973, MBTA acquired PC's commuter rail property, and in 1975 and 1976, it acquired B&M's rolling stock and property. In both situations, the railroads continued to supply services. Conrail assumed operation of PC's services in 1976 but only served as an MBTA operator for one year. In 1977, MBTA contracted B&M as operator of all suburban heavy-rail services; an arrangement continued until 1987 when Amtrak was awarded operation

Continued on page 124.

Continued on from page 120.

of MBTA commuter services. In 2003, MBTA changed operators again, awarding commuter rail operations to the newly formed Massachusetts Bay Commuter Railroad Company, a consortium that included experienced rail operator Veolia.

Beginning in the mid-1970s, MBTA bought replacement equipment for suburban services. To save money, it opted for rebuilt and secondhand equipment until funds became available for new equipment built specifically for its needs. Under MBTA, Boston's commuter rail has enjoyed an expanded route structure and more frequent services. Significantly, a number of routes have been restored to service, and multimodal transportation hubs have been built to facilitate transfer from heavy rail to urban transit.

METRO-NORTH TO CONNECTICUT AND JERSEY

Metro-North is the operating subsidiary of the Metropolitan Transportation Authority providing services on former New Haven Railroad and New York Central System routes radiating north from Grand Central Terminal and also coordinating with NJ Transit services to Port Jervis, New York, on the former Erie Railroad from Hoboken, New Jersey. In the aftermath of Penn Central bankruptcy, MTA assumed financial responsibility for the New York portion of these services, with the Connecticut Department of Transportation (ConnDOT) supporting Connecticut operations on former New Haven Lines.

One aspect of MTA's influence was purchase of new Metropolitan series electric multiple-units, derived from the same pattern as cars recently designed for LIRR. During the early phase of MTA/ConnDOT involvement, Penn Central remained as the operator until Conrail assumed operations on April 1, 1976. Some equipment, such as former New Haven FL9s (specialized diesel-electric/third-rail electric locomotives for New York City services), was lettered for Conrail. When Conrail exited the commuter business at the end of 1982, Metro-North began operating its own trains and took possession of Conrail's FL9s and other equipment.

COMMUTER SERVICES IN THE NATION'S RAIL HUB

Chicago's private-public suburban service transition began a decade later than in eastern cities. The city's Regional Transportation Authority was established to oversee suburban services in 1973, and its first major task came in 1975 and 1976, when Rock Island's bankruptcy forced the RTA to assume responsibility for the Rock's LaSalle Street Station–based commuter services to Joliet. This proved an interim step toward becoming a railroad operator. In 1982, RTA formed the Northeast Illinois Railroad Corporation, which took over operations of former Rock Island and Milwaukee Road Chicago–based commuter services.

During 1983 and 1984, RTA adopted the name Metra for Chicago's suburban rail operations. The Metra branding has been applied to the majority of Chicago's surviving

commuter rail operations, including services on former Burlington, Chicago & North Western, Illinois Central, Milwaukee Road, Rock Island, and Wabash routes. However, while Metra has assumed ownership of equipment and operation of most services, some services are still contracted to host railroads, notably BNSF over the former Burlington triple-track to Aurora. In 1996, Metra began a new service using Wisconsin Central Limited's former Soo Line route, the first all-new Chicago suburban expansion since Metra's involvement in regional commuter rail.

SP'S CALIFORNIA COMMUTES

For decades, Southern Pacific's San Francisco–San Jose Peninsula "Commutes" (not known as "commuter trains") were the only intensive heavy-rail suburban services in the West. The route had enjoyed continuous passenger service since the opening of the San Francisco & San Jose Railroad in 1863 and remains the busiest single suburban line west of Chicago.

SP retained its Commute service after May 1, 1971, when Amtrak assumed operation of all its long-distance passenger trains. In 1975 SP petitioned the ICC to abandon the Commute service, setting in motion the process of public agencies assuming operations. In 1980, the California Department of Transportation (Caltrans) stepped in by providing local funding

A colorful era in New York commuter rail: on April 27, 1984, a Metro-North train of SEMTA (Southeastern Michigan Transportation Authority) coaches led by a former Conrail B23-7 and FL9 approaches 125th Street Station in Harlem. Although primarily a bus operator, between 1974 and 1983 SEMTA provided a limited suburban rail service between Pontiac and Detroit on Grand Trunk Western. When this service ended, equipment-strapped Metro-North took advantage of the surplus cars, while SEMTA's GP9 locomotives went to MBTA. *Walter E. Zullig Jr.*

Metro-North Timeline

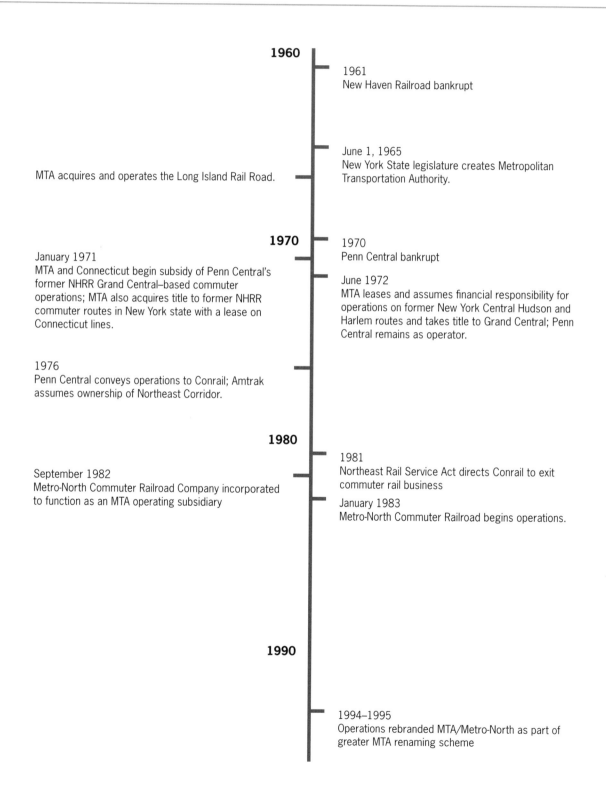

1960

1961
New Haven Railroad bankrupt

June 1, 1965
New York State legislature creates Metropolitan
Transportation Authority.

MTA acquires and operates the Long Island Rail Road.

1970

1970
Penn Central bankrupt

January 1971
MTA and Connecticut begin subsidy of Penn Central's
former NHRR Grand Central–based commuter
operations; MTA also acquires title to former NHRR
commuter routes in New York state with a lease on
Connecticut lines.

June 1972
MTA leases and assumes financial responsibility for
operations on former New York Central Hudson and
Harlem routes and takes title to Grand Central; Penn
Central remains as operator.

1976
Penn Central conveys operations to Conrail; Amtrak
assumes ownership of Northeast Corridor.

1980

1981
Northeast Rail Service Act directs Conrail to exit
commuter rail business

September 1982
Metro-North Commuter Railroad Company incorporated
to function as an MTA operating subsidiary

January 1983
Metro-North Commuter Railroad begins operations.

1990

1994–1995
Operations rebranded MTA/Metro-North as part of
greater MTA renaming scheme

secured from San Francisco, San Mateo, and San Jose counties. During the first five years of Caltrans' involvement, trains and services were essentially the same as they had been under SP ownership while SP remained the contract operator. This changed dramatically in 1985 when Caltrans procured new Japanese-built, stainless-steel, bi-level, push-pull gallery cars and 18 new EMD F40PH diesel-electrics. With this equipment, the Caltrain brand replaced SP's name.

Transition to public operation reached the next stage with formation of the Peninsula Corridor Joint Powers Board in 1987. By this time SP was willing to discuss divesting its Peninsula Line, and in 1991, the new agency was able acquire SP's San Francisco–San Jose route along with trackage rights on SP's Coast Line to Gilroy. Then, in 1992, the Joint Powers Board contracted Amtrak to replace SP as a contract operator. Since that time increased highway congestion and rising public demand for rail transit has led Caltrain to implement significant infrastructure and service improvements.

An ACE (Altamont Commuter Express) train passes the nature refuge at Alviso, California, on its run from San Jose to Stockton. The ACE trains are among the most obscure passenger services in California with just four round trips daily via its namesake mountain pass. ACE is a modern-day creation, so unlike traditional suburban railway operations it has no historical antecedent. However, a portion of the ACE route uses Union Pacific's former Western Pacific mainline that once hosted the famed *California Zephyr*. *Brian Solomon*

Chicago METRA Timeline

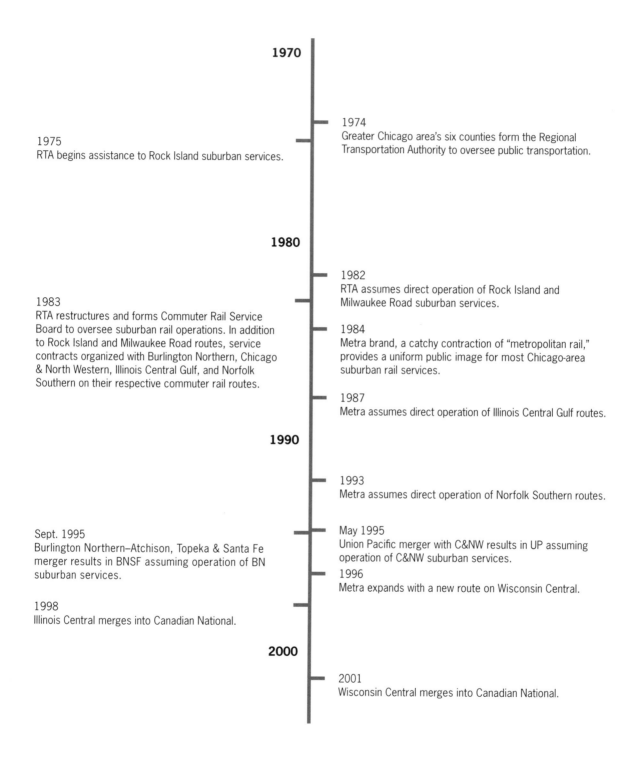

1970

1974
Greater Chicago area's six counties form the Regional Transportation Authority to oversee public transportation.

1975
RTA begins assistance to Rock Island suburban services.

1980

1982
RTA assumes direct operation of Rock Island and Milwaukee Road suburban services.

1983
RTA restructures and forms Commuter Rail Service Board to oversee suburban rail operations. In addition to Rock Island and Milwaukee Road routes, service contracts organized with Burlington Northern, Chicago & North Western, Illinois Central Gulf, and Norfolk Southern on their respective commuter rail routes.

1984
Metra brand, a catchy contraction of "metropolitan rail," provides a uniform public image for most Chicago-area suburban rail services.

1987
Metra assumes direct operation of Illinois Central Gulf routes.

1990

1993
Metra assumes direct operation of Norfolk Southern routes.

Sept. 1995
Burlington Northern–Atchison, Topeka & Santa Fe merger results in BNSF assuming operation of BN suburban services.

May 1995
Union Pacific merger with C&NW results in UP assuming operation of C&NW suburban services.

1996
Metra expands with a new route on Wisconsin Central.

1998
Illinois Central merges into Canadian National.

2000

2001
Wisconsin Central merges into Canadian National.

Caltrain Timeline

1970

1971
Amtrak assumes operation of Southern Pacific long-distance passenger services; SP retains San Francisco–San Jose commute service.

1977
SP petitions to discontinue Peninsula commute service.

1980

1980
Caltrans assumes oversight of Peninsula commute service; SP serves as contract operator.

1985
Caltrans purchases new equipment replacing SP-era trains; new trains lettered for Caltrain.

1987
Santa Clara, San Mateo, and San Francisco counties form the Peninsula Corridor Joint Powers Board (JPB).

1990

1991
JPB acquires primary commuter rail properties from SP.

1992
JPB assumes full management and operation of Caltrain commutes and contracts train operation to Amtrak; trains retain Caltrain branding.

1996
SP merges with Union Pacific.

2000

2010

2012
JPB contracts Transit America Services to operate Caltrain services.

NEW CALIFORNIA SERVICES

Since a public referendum to support rail transport in 1990, California has had a public mandate to improve rail services. In addition to existing Amtrak and Caltrain services, state and local communities have worked with private railroads (initially Santa Fe, SP, and UP) to acquire railway lines and operating rights while establishing new railway agencies to operate passenger trains. Intermediate-distance intercity services come under provisions of the Amtrak charter, with Amtrak providing services and California providing most equipment and subsidies. Thus, the locomotives and cars are lettered for Amtrak California, special-ordered for California's service requirements.

Altamont Commuter Express Joint Power Authority was formed by regional agencies for the purpose of providing service between Stockton and San Jose on a route that had no history of suburban service. Trains are known as Altamont Commuter Express because they run via Altamont Pass. Service began in October 1998. Trains are operated and maintained under contract by Herzog Transit Services.

In 1991, the Southern California Regional Rail Authority was formed as joint authority of five participating counties in greater Los Angeles, negotiating purchase arrangements for lines or trackage rights from all three of the three major freight railroads in the LA area. Passenger services were named Metrolink and Amtrak was contracted as initial operator. Metrolink began operations on October 26, 1992, and gradually expanded service.

The San Diego area's North County Transit District began Coaster brand suburban services on the former Santa Fe Surf Line in 1995. In 2008, NCTD began Sprinter brand services using European-style lightweight diesel railcars on the former Santa Fe Escondido Branch.

Chapter 6

PLANNED SYSTEMS AND THE FUTURE

When American railroads were returned to private ownership after World War I, several serious concepts emerged for mass railroad consolidation in the United States. The ICC was directed to oversee consolidation efforts. Various plans were proposed to improve efficiency and reduce undesirable competition while building stronger and healthier networks.

During the Great Depression, as railroads faced drastic declines in traffic and revenue, the Prince Plan offered cost efficiencies aimed at rejuvenating the industry. Sponsored by Boston banker Frederick H. Prince, the plan was drafted in 1933 by John W. Barriger III (renowned for his later career, in which he embraced innovative management to bring ailing railroads renewed prosperity). Initially, the Prince Plan favored eight regional networks, four in the East and four in the West, but later was scaled back to seven networks featuring just three in the West.

Like earlier proposed groupings, such as the Oldham Plan and the Ripley Reports, the Prince Plan was never adopted (not only did it rely on voluntary amalgamations between different lines, hopes of its implementation were doomed because elements of the proposal were opposed both by railroad labor and management). Barriger's groupings, however, offered fascinating alternatives and its similarities to how American railroad systems ultimately developed make for interesting comparisons. The cores of the seven systems were based on the New York Central (System 1), Pennsylvania Railroad (System 2), Atlantic Coast Line and Louisville & Nashville (System 3), Southern Railway and Illinois Central (System 4), the Hill Lines (System 5), Union Pacific and Southern Pacific (System 6), and the Santa Fe and Missouri Pacific (System 7).

Barriger's networks were designed to improve railroad efficiency by focusing traffic on principal routes and deliberately pared parallel routes in an effort to reduce mainline redundancy while maintaining competition through primary gateways. In studying his railroad groupings, it appears that the end result would have eliminated or at least minimized the importance of

Today, Union Pacific is one of two massive western railroads. On the evening of August 14, 2009, a westward UP freight glides down grade through California's Feather River Canyon, the route built by the George Gould a century ago to fulfill his dreams for a unified transcontinental line. Yet, as of early 2013, railroads in the United States maintain the long standing east-west regional divide. Will an ultimate merger finally allow one carrier to span the whole country? *Brian Solomon*

select secondary gateways such as Buffalo, the Twin Cities, and the Twin Ports of Duluth and Superior, while allowing for consolidation of main routes, especially in the East and Midwest. The groupings largely adhered to preexisting or traditional family arrangements, but in a few cases Barriger divided existing companies to better suit regional system partitions or to provide necessary balance in the new systems.

His choices for Systems 3 and 5 appear to have benefited from prescient or undeniable logic, since as proposed these systems closely resemble the 1970s- and 1980s-era Seaboard System and Burlington Northern systems. By contrast, his Northeast groupings offer a very different map than what developed.

Fundamental shifts in regulatory policy, economic motives, and corporate paradigms have doomed most predictions of railroad realignment. None of the plans of the 1920s or 1930s paired Pennsylvania Railroad and New York Central. At the time, such a combination was inconceivable, and yet, in the 1960s it became reality (but for unsound reasons). Will future railroad merger planners find ways to look beyond today's merger taboos? Will they learn from the lesson of Penn Central or will they be doomed to repeat it? Will railroads continue to get bigger or will they break up into smaller units?

MERGERS THAT NEVER WILL BE

As long as there are two or more railroad companies, there exists opportunity for merger, or as demonstrated with the breakup of Conrail, division of existing systems. It is impossible to predict the future. Just ask the planners of Santa Fe Southern Pacific.

Over the years there have been rumors, discussions, and plans regarding many combinations that never came to pass. In the late 1940s, for example, Lackawanna hoped to merge with Nickel Plate Road. In the early 1960s Southern Pacific and Santa Fe both approached Western Pacific, yet neither combination was consummated. Instead, two decades later, WP joined the Union Pacific system. UP and Rock Island went through the motions of merger in the 1960s, and while the union was approved by the ICC, the decision had taken too long, by which time Rock Island had fallen into such a poor state that UP backed out. Ultimately, the Rock was liquidated, its system dismembered, and its equipment sold. (Today, many of Rock's surviving lines are part of the UP system, mostly through its acquisition of SP, C&NW, and other lines.) In the 1970s, Santa Fe considered buying Erie Lackawanna, a union that would have made for America's first true transcon. It's understood that EL's money-losing commuter lines, high terminal costs, and expensive crew arrangements discouraged Santa Fe from further pursuing this unorthodox union.

When the UP-SP combination was discussed in the mid-1990s, some Conrail officials considered making a bid for SP's Cotton Belt routes on the premise that Conrail could offer

Continued on page 136.

Overleaf: Today's Wheeling & Lake Erie regional railroad operates a vestige of George Gould's vision. In August 2011, a W&LE extra freight crosses the massive former Pittsburgh & West Virginia bridge at Speers, Pennsylvania, as an empty CSX coal train roars below at river level. *Brian Solomon*

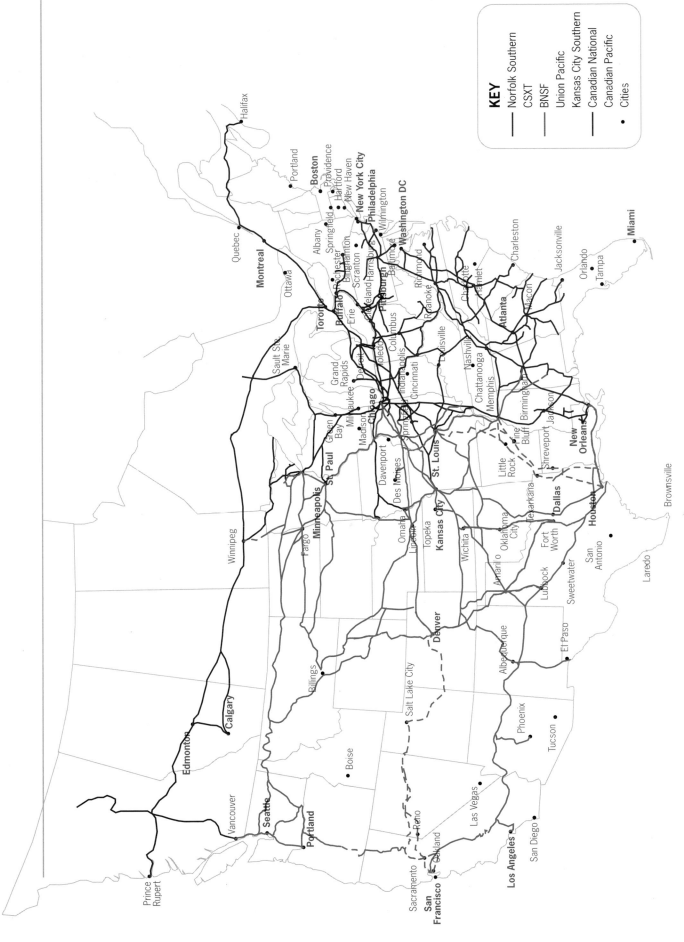

Norfolk Southern, BNSF, and Canadian National

Map by Brian Solomon © 2013

KEY
- Norfolk Southern
- CSXT
- BNSF
- Union Pacific
- Kansas City Southern
- Canadian National
- Canadian Pacific
- • Cities

Continued from page 132.

competition to an unchecked UP-SP near monopoly in the petrochemical markets of Louisiana and Texas. Conrail plus Cotton Belt would have created a very different rail map than Conrail's subsequent partition by NS and CSX in the late 1990s.

What if the STB had given the nod to the proposed BNSF-CN megamerger of 1999 and 2000? Surely this would have set off a wave of "final" mergers among the major players. Perhaps Union Pacific and CSX would have merged, and Norfolk Southern, KCS, and CP Rail would have joined forces, forming three massive transcontinental rail systems.

AN EYE ON THE FUTURE

What lies ahead? If history gives us any clue we can expect more changes in railroading. Since the industry's formative days, companies have made alliances, controlled and leased prospective partners, and merged to make bigger companies. As of 2013, the industry has enjoyed a remarkable period of stability since the merger frenzy of the 1980s and 1990s completely redrew the map. The American Association of Railroads, which compiles data on railroads operating in the Unites States, reports that in 2011 there were seven Class I carriers, further noting that the two largest Canadian railroads and two largest Mexican lines would qualify as Class I lines if operating in the United States.

Over the years the Class I qualification has changed, so lines that would have been deemed Class I carriers decades ago, might be too small today. As of 2011, the principal qualification was an annual operating revenue threshold of $433.2 million. Only BNSF, CSXT, GT Corp (Canadian National's U.S. operations affiliate), Kansas City Southern, Norfolk Southern, Soo Line (Canadian Pacific's U.S. operations affiliate), and Union Pacific make this list. Other railroads with significant mileage, such as Florida East Coast, Montana Rail Link, and Pan Am Railways, fall into the Class II category. Of the 138,565-route-mile network in the United States, 95,514 miles are operated by the seven Class I railroads, yet in 2012 a total of 567 railroad companies were operational in the United States. Significantly, based on 2009 traffic figures, railroads in the United States carried nearly three times the ton-miles that the network handled in 1950. This simple fact might lend credence to the 1930s philosophy regarding the concentration of tonnage on fewer lines. It certainly indicates that the American economy has grown. Since much of the gain has occurred after passage of the 1980s Staggers Act, this growth appears to demonstrate the positive effect of deregulation on railroad traffic.

But what clues do these facts give us about the future? Since the last wave of major mergers that concluded with the divide of Conrail, the big railroads have largely focused on the business of running trains. The smaller companies have continued to merge and make changes. Among the most notable trend has been the growth of short-line operators. Today, many of the most significant short-line and regional railways are operated by just a handful companies. The

most recent merger was Genesee & Wyoming's acquisition of RailAmerica at the end of 2012, putting more than 110 small- and medium-size railroads under one helm. But unlike Union Pacific or the other massive Class I lines, G&W consists of numerous disconnected lines, some beyond North American shores.

Will there be big bombshell mergers when the big players decide to make the move? Will railroads continue to combine, or alternatively will the big networks be deemed unmanageable and spun off into smaller, leaner companies?

There have been rumors and mumblings of mergers and changes from time to time, but the most significant combinations are usually kept quiet until the prospective parties are ready to make their announcements. Perhaps backroom discussions between railroad executives are poised to redraw the map again, and at any moment a joint press release will announce an industry shake up. Or maybe executives believe that regulatory bodies are unfavorable to megamergers and will continue with business as usual.

POTENTIAL PARTNERS

Unlike the Canadian railroads, American railroad mergers have avoided true transcontinental combinations. Industry observers have offered a variety of reasons precluding the benefits of a true United States coast-to-coast transcon. Traditional railroads have feared that such a union might result in the freezing out of excluded parties from established interchange traffic. For

A vision of modern railroading: Kansas City Southern and BNSF SD70ACe diesel-electrics work together on a unit coal train traversing the KCS mainline near South Dorsey, Arkansas. Will KCS continue to remain independent, or will it eventually merge with one of the larger Class I railroads? *Brian Solomon*

example, if NS and BNSF merge, the combined railroad might lose out on traffic previously exchanged between BNSF and CSX, and NS and UP (not to mention the Canadian roads).

The nature of transcontinental traffic is that it originates and terminates at myriad points on opposite sides of the country. Since carload traffic has to be classified at least once anyway, and single-commodity unit trains and intermodal traffic already benefit from run-through arrangements, the cost savings of a transcontinental system don't appear a sufficient incentive for railroads to make the big leap. However, don't exclude the effect of executive ego on potential merger schemes. What drove George Gould to try for a transcontinental network 110 years ago? It certainly doesn't appear to have been traffic!

Since the major systems are more or less balanced against one another, mergers between BNSF and UP or CSX and NS appear out of the question, based on contemporary concepts of necessary competition.

OPEN ACCESS

Step back a moment and consider the less obvious motives behind change within the industry. How could elements of railroading result in radical change? What if the "paper barriers" preventing interchange between lines that are otherwise physically connected are eliminated? Presently, various arrangements stemming from mergers and line sales limit which lines may interchange traffic. If these agreements—the paper barriers—are voided, it opens the field in ways not considered today. Furthermore, what if shippers successfully demand open access, a move that could allow railroads to reach beyond traditional limitations of their owned infrastructures. Some railroad executives cringe at the very mention of such a concept.

Across Europe open access rules have changed the way freight is moved. Dozens of new operators have sprouted up to serve the needs of customers, while the separation of freight and passenger operations from infrastructure has allowed mergers between previously nationalized freight operators. The German freight operator DB merged with national freight operators in the Netherlands and Denmark, bought EWS from Canadian National (thus DB serves customers across the United Kingdom), and is part owner of Swiss BLS Cargo and other transport and logistics firms. (DB's acquisition of and merger with trucking firm Schenker produced the present DB Schenker name.) The concept translated to American railroads could result in Class I carriers reaching well beyond their present infrastructural limits and negotiated trackage rights, and enable short lines to legally solicit traffic from customers reached by tracks owned by a Class I railroad. Theoretically, the Podunk & Eastern could reach cross-country to tap a customer on another line.

The logistics of how to pay for track usage, as well as which companies would provide and qualify crews and supply locomotives and rolling stock, along with other issues, would

Continued on page 148.

Future Merger Scenario 1

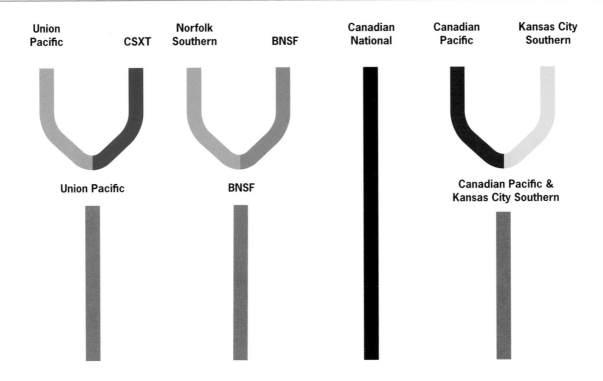

Future Merger Scenario 2

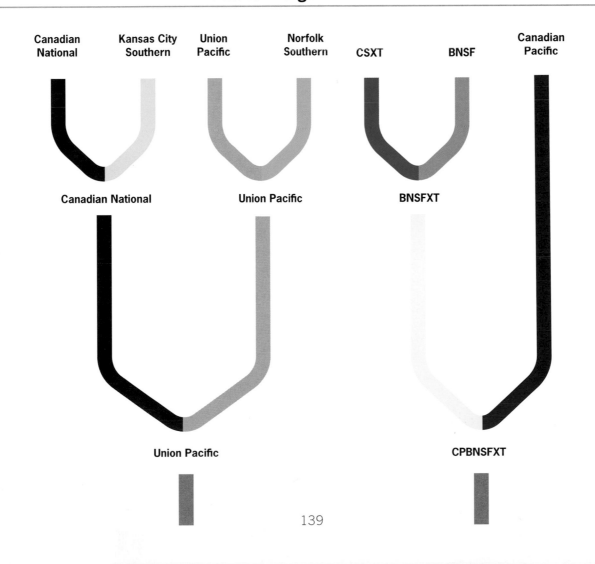

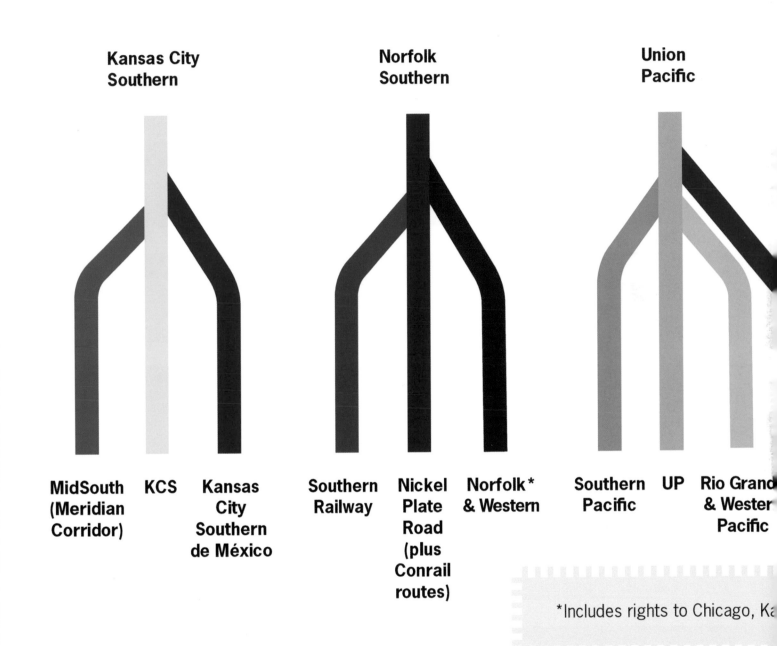

Kansas City Southern

MidSouth (Meridian Corridor) • KCS • Kansas City Southern de México

Norfolk Southern

Southern Railway • Nickel Plate Road (plus Conrail routes) • Norfolk* & Western

Union Pacific

Southern Pacific • UP • Rio Grande & Western Pacific

*Includes rights to Chicago, Ka

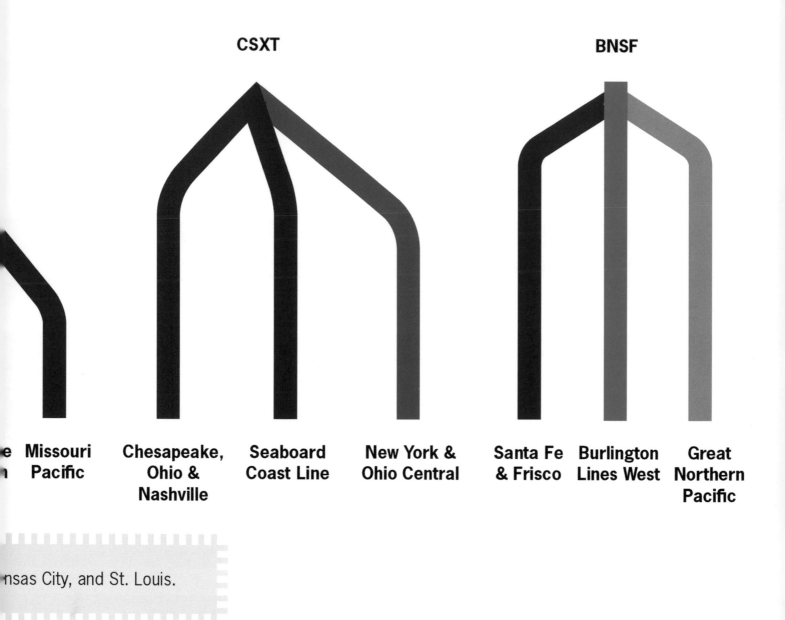

Missouri
Pacific

Chesapeake,
Ohio &
Nashville

Seaboard
Coast Line

New York &
Ohio Central

Santa Fe
& Frisco

Burlington
Lines West

Great
Northern
Pacific

CSXT

BNSF

nsas City, and St. Louis.

144

Future Merger Scenario 3

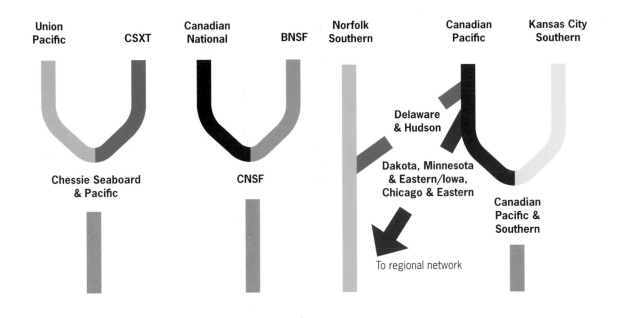

Union
Pacific   CSXT

Canadian
National   BNSF

Norfolk
Southern

Canadian
Pacific

Kansas City
Southern

Chessie Seaboard
& Pacific

CNSF

Delaware
& Hudson

Dakota, Minnesota
& Eastern/Iowa,
Chicago & Eastern

To regional network

Canadian
Pacific &
Southern

Future Merger Scenario 4

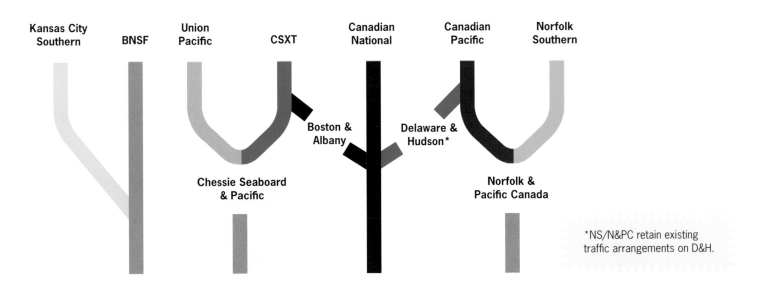

Kansas City
Southern   BNSF

Union
Pacific   CSXT

Canadian
National

Canadian
Pacific

Norfolk
Southern

Chessie Seaboard
& Pacific

Boston &
Albany

Delaware &
Hudson*

Norfolk &
Pacific Canada

*NS/N&PC retain existing
traffic arrangements on D&H.

On a blazing August 2011 morning, a modern Evolution Series General Electric diesel leads a BNSF unit potash train east on the old Frisco system at Richland, Missouri. While big railroads and unit trains offer efficient movement of bulk goods, have massive railroads such as BNSF lost the ability to realize profits from small shipments? Might regional systems be more effective for smaller shippers? *Brian Solomon*

Future Merger Scenario 5

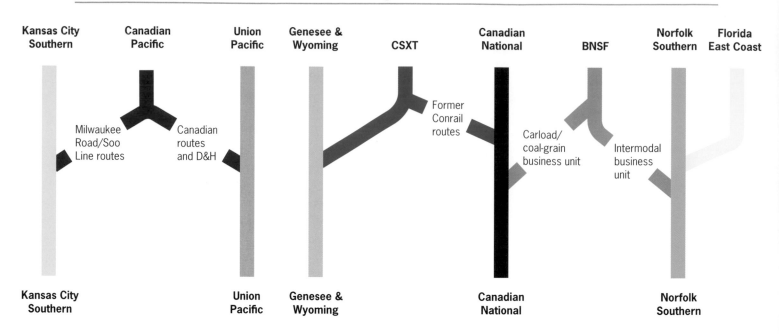

| Kansas City Southern | Canadian Pacific | Union Pacific | Genesee & Wyoming | CSXT | Canadian National | BNSF | Norfolk Southern | Florida East Coast |

Milwaukee Road/Soo Line routes

Canadian routes and D&H

Former Conrail routes

Carload/ coal-grain business unit

Intermodal business unit

| Kansas City Southern | | Union Pacific | Genesee & Wyoming | | Canadian National | | Norfolk Southern | |

In 2012, the Norfolk Southern celebrated the 30th anniversary of its merger between the Norfolk and Western and Southern Railway. As part of that celebration 20 new AC traction locomotives were painted in modern adaptations of predecessor's liveries designed by famed railway artist Andy Fletcher. All 20 specially painted locomotives were gathered for a family portrait at the former Southern Railway roundhouse (now the North Carolina Transportation Museum) in Spencer, North Carolina, over the July 4, 2012, holiday. *Patrick Yough*

Future Merger Scenario 6

Zhongguo Tielu (China Railways)
Union Pacific
Kansas City Southern
BNSF
Montana Rail Link
CSXT
Canadian National
Canadian Pacific
SBB Cargo
Norfolk Southern
DB Schenker USA

China Railways East Pacific Division

Berkshire Railways

Canadian National

SBB Cargo North America

DB Schenker USA

Continued from page 138.

need to be resolved. Following a European model would relieve some of the complexity of an American open-access arrangement. Obviously, the large, well-established freight railroads might have the most to lose by such a proposal and strenuously object to such arrangements. Yet, stranger changes have occurred in the world of railroading. Open access might result in a host of new services or it might doom the industry through parasitic competition. Keep in mind, railroading survived the changes brought on by deregulation and thrived despite some dire predictions of doom beforehand.

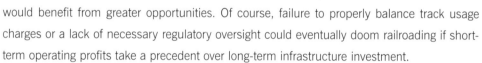

One result of open access might be a rearrangement of the roles various railroad companies play. A company with excellent infrastructure and a good traffic base that suffers from constipated operations might find it more lucrative to focus on the infrastructure side of the business while leaving operations to a more adept company. If access charges are adequately structured to reward each player, everyone involved could benefit. The infrastructure railroad would earn more from improved utilization, and the operator would have the freedom to serve customers across the North American network, maximizing the use of equipment. Meanwhile, customers would benefit from improved service and the labor pool would benefit from greater opportunities. Of course, failure to properly balance track usage charges or a lack of necessary regulatory oversight could eventually doom railroading if short-term operating profits take a precedent over long-term infrastructure investment.

Will America consider open access? When most world railways were nationalized state-run operations, the United States largely relied on private industry to operate its railroads. Based on this history, it seems unlikely that the United States will follow international trends and adopt the alternative open-access arrangements popular in Europe.

RESTRUCTURING ROUTE STRUCTURES

On another front, must American railroads continue to be limited by their antique route structure? Very few new routes have been added to the American map since before World War I. (One of the few exceptions was Burlington Northern's and Chicago & North Western's penetration of Wyoming's Powder River Basin in the 1970s and 1980s, where enormous traffic potential allowed for unprecedented late-era expansion.) What if the cost of new line construction became affordable again, giving private railroads the ability to fill gaps in the network while building new lines to reach new markets?

What if state and federal governments began funding all-new freight and passenger routes that allow railroads to open new corridors and tap new traffic? Again, if North American railroads look to their European and Chinese counterparts, there are many possibilities for change. In Switzerland and Austria long-term strategies include construction of exceptionally long Alpine tunnels that will revolutionize the ability of existing railways to move freight. What if a 50-mile tunnel were constructed below the California Tehachapis? This would eliminate the present bottleneck caused by an exceptionally sinuous line saddled with sections of single-track that limits the flow of freight and precludes practical operation of inland passenger services. In the 1930s, Baltimore & Ohio contemplated a low-grade super railroad across central Pennsylvania. If such a line were built today how would it effect operations in the future?

How might rising fuel costs affect railroad transport? Railroads enjoy greater efficiency than highways, but how will continued industrial decline as result of rising fuel costs affect traffic? Likewise, how might a more efficient rail-freight network benefit American industry? New rail-based technologies that lower the cost of transport might attract traffic to routes in ways we cannot imagine. New technology, new traffic, new regulations, and other changes may transform American railways in ways beyond our present imaginations.

The colorful era of 1950s railroad has been reinvented through NS's heritage paint liveries on its modern diesels. Where just seven large railroads now dominate modern freight railroading, prior to the frenzied merger movement beginning in the late 1950s, dozens of carriers operated American railroads. Virginian, Wabash, and the Interstate Railroad are just a few of the names lost in the waves of railroad mergers. *Patrick Yough*

Conrail predecessors Penn Central, Erie Railroad, and Delaware, Lackawanna & Western vanished a generation before the advent of the modern safety-cab, yet Norfolk Southern's faithful renditions of these historic paint schemes on modern locomotives give us a hint of what might have been. *Patrick Yough*

BIBLIOGRAPHY

BOOKS

1846–1896 Fiftieth Anniversary of the Incorporation of the Pennsylvania Railroad Company. Philadelphia 1896.

A Century of Progress—History of the Delaware and Hudson Company 1823–1923. Delaware & Hudson, Albany, New York, 1925.

All Stations: A Journey Through 150 Years of Railway History. Paris, 1978.

Encyclopedia of American Business History and Biography: Railroads in the Nineteenth Century. Bruccoli Clark Layman, Inc., and Facts on File, Inc., 1988.

The American Railway—Its Construction, Development, Management, and Appliances. New York, 1893.

Anderson, Craig T. *Amtrak—the National Rail Passenger Corporation 1978-1979 Annual.* San Francisco, 1978.

Anderson, Elaine. *The Central Railroad of New Jersey's First 100 Years.* Center for Canal History and Technology. Easton, PA, 1984.

Archer, Robert F. *A History of the Lehigh Valley Railroad—Route of the Black Diamond.* Berkeley, CA, 1977.

Asay, Jeff S. *Track and Time—an Operational History of the Western Pacific Railroad through Timetables and Maps.* Portola, CA, 2006.

Baedeker, Karl. *Baedeker's The United States—Handbook for Travelers.* Leipzig, Germany, 1909.

Bancroft, Hubert Howe. *History of California,* vol. 7. San Francisco, 1890.

Berton, Pierre. *The Last Spike: The Great Railway 1881–1885.* Toronto, 1971.

Bezilla, Michael. *Electric Traction on the Pennsylvania Railroad 1895–1968.* State College, PA, 1981.

Black, Robert C., III. *The Railroads of the Confederacy.* Chapel Hill, NC, 1952.

Bradley, Rodger. *Amtrak—The US National Railroad Passenger Corporation.* Dorset, UK, 1985.

Bryant, Keith L. *History of the Atchison, Topeka and Santa Fe Railway.* New York, 1974.

Bryant, Keith L., Jr. *Railroads in the Age of Regulation, 1900–1980.* New York, 1988.

Burgess, George, H., and Miles C. Kennedy. *Centennial History of the Pennsylvania Railroad.* Philadelphia, 1949.

Burke, Davis. *The Southern Railway—Road of the Innovators.* Chapel Hill, NC, 1985.

Byron, Carl R. *A Pinprick of Light, The Troy and Greenfield Railroad and Its Hoosac Tunnel.* Shelburne, VT, 1995.

Casey, Robert J., and W. A. S. Douglas. *The Lackawanna Story.* New York, 1951.

Chernow, Ron. *The House of Morgan.* New York, 1990.

Churella, Albert, J. *From Steam to Diesel.* Princeton, NJ, 1998.

Condit, Carl, *Port of New York,* vols. 1 & 2. Chicago, 1980, 1981.

Cupper, Dan. *Horseshoe Heritage, The Story of a Great Railroad Landmark.* Halifax, PA, 1996.

Currie, A.W. *The Grand Trunk Railway of Canada.* Toronto, 1957.

Daggett, Stuart. *History of the Southern Pacific.* New York, 1922.

Daughen, Joseph R., and Peter Binzen. *The Wreck of the Penn Central*. Boston, 1971.

Del Grosso, Robert C. *Burlington Northern 1980–1991 Annual*. Denver, 1991.

Doherty, Timothy Scott, and Brian Solomon. *Conrail*. St. Paul, MN., 2004.

Dolzall, Gary W., and Stephen F. Dolzall. *Monon—The Hoosier Line*. Glendale, CA, 1987.

Dorsey, Edward Bates. *English and American Railroads Compared*. New York, 1887.

Droege, John A. *Freight Terminals and Trains*. New York, 1912.

————. *Passenger Terminals and Trains*. New York, 1916.

Drury, George H. *Guide to North American Steam Locomotives*. Waukesha, WI, 1993.

————. *The Historical Guide to North American Railroads*. Waukesha, WI, 1985.

————. *The Train Watcher's Guide to North American Railroads*. Waukesha, WI, 1992.

Dunscomb, Guy, L. *A Century of Southern Pacific Steam Locomotives*. Modesto, CA, 1963.

Farrington, S. Kip, Jr. *Railroading from the Head End*. New York, 1943.

————. *Railroading from the Rear End*. New York, 1946.

————. *Railroading the Modern Way*. New York, 1951.

————. *Railroads at War*. New York, 1944.

————. *Railroads of the Hour*. New York, 1958.

————. *Railroads of Today*. New York, 1949.

Fitzsimons, Bernard. *150 Years of Canadian Railroads*. Toronto, 1984.

Frailey, Fred W. *Zephyrs, Chiefs & Other Orphans—The First Five Years of Amtrak*. Godfrey, IL, 1977.

Frey, Robert L. *Railroads in the Nineteenth Century*. New York, 1988.

Garmany, John B. *Southern Pacific Dieselization*. Edmonds, WA, 1985.

Glischinski, Steve. *Burlington Northern and its Heritage*. Andover, New Jersey. and Osceola, WI, 1996.

Grant, H. Roger. *Erie Lackawanna—Death of an American Railroad, 1938–1992*. Stanford, CA, 1994.

Grodinsky, Julius. *Jay Gould—His Business Career 1867–1892*. Philadelphia, 1957.

Gruber, John. *Railroad History in a Nutshell*. Madison, WI, 2009.

————. *Railroad Preservation in a Nutshell*. Madison, WI, 2011.

Gruber, John, and Brian Solomon. *The Milwaukee Road's Hiawathas*. St. Paul, MN, 2006.

Hampton, Taylor. *The Nickel Plate Road*. Cleveland, OH, 1947.

Hare, Jay V. *History of the Reading*. Philadelphia, PA, 1966.

Harlow, Alvin F. *The Road of the Century*. New York, 1947.

————. *Steelways of New England*. New York, 1946.

Hayes, William Edward. *Iron Road to Empire—The History of the Rock Island Lines*. 1953.

Heath, Erle. *Seventy-Five Years of Progress—Historical Sketch of the Southern Pacific*. San Francisco, 1945.

Hedges, James Blaine. *Henry Villard and the Railways of the Northwest*. New York, 1930.

Helmer, William F. *O&W—The Long Life and Slow Death of the New York, Ontario & Western Ry*, 2nd ed. San Diego, CA, 1959.

Hidy, Ralph W., Muriel E. Hidy, Roy V. Scott, with Don L. Hofsommer. *The Great Northern Railway*. Boston, 1988.

Hilton, George W. *American Narrow Gauge Railroads*. Stanford, CA, 1990.

Hofsommer, Don. L. *Southern Pacific 1900–1985*. College Station, TX, 1986.

Holbrook, Stewart H. *James J. Hill*. New York, 1955.

————. *The Story of American Railroads*. New York, 1947.

Holland, Rupert Sargent. *Historic Railroads*. Philadelphia, 1927.

Hollander, Stanley, C. *Passenger Transportation*. Lansing, MI, 1968.

Hoyt, Edwin P. *The Vanderbilts and their Fortunes*. New York, 1962.

Hungerford, Edward. *Daniel Willard Rides the Line*. New York, 1938.

————. *Men of Erie*. New York, n.d.

Ivey, Paul Wesley. *The Pere Marquette Railroad Company*. 1970.

Johnson, Emory, R. *Railway Transportation*. New York, 1910.

Jones, Robert C. *The Central Vermont Railway*, vols. 1–7. Shelburne, VT, 1995.

Jones, Robert W. *Boston & Albany: The New York Central in New England*, vols. 1 and 2. Los Angeles, 1997.

Karr, Ronald Dale. *The Rail Lines of Southern New England*. Pepperell, MA, 1995.

Keilty, Edmund. *Interurbans Without Wires*. Glendale, CA, 1979.

King, Steve. *Clinchfield Country*. Silver Spring, MD, 1988.

Klein, Maury. *History of the Louisville & Nashville Railroad*. New York, 1972.

————. *Union Pacific*, vols. 1 and 2. New York, 1989.

————. *Union Pacific: The Reconfiguration; American's Greatest Railroad from 1969 to the Present*. Oxford, NY, 2011.

Lamb, W. Kaye. *History of the Canadian Pacific Railway*. New York, 1977.

Latham, Earl. *The Politics of Railroad Coordination 1933–1936*. Cambridge, MA, 1959

LeMassena, Robert A. *Colorado's Mountain Railroads*. Golden, CO, 1963.

————. *Rio Grande to the Pacific*. Denver, 1974

Lemly, James H. *The Gulf, Mobile & Ohio*. Homewood, IL, 1953.

Leopard, John. *Wisconsin Central Heritage*, vol. 2. La Mirada, CA, 2008.

Lewis, Oscar. *The Big Four*. New York, 1938.

Malone, Michael P. *James J. Hill, Empire Builder of the Northwest*. Norman, OK, 1996.

Marshall, James. *Santa Fe—The Railroad That Built an Empire*. New York, 1945.

McLean, Harold H. *Pittsburgh & Lake Erie Railroad*. Golden West Books, San Marino, CA, 1980.

Middleton, William D. *Grand Central . . . the World's Greatest Railway Terminal*. San Marino, CA, 1977.

————. *Landmarks on the Iron Road*. Bloomington, IN, 1999.

————. *When the Steam Railroads Electrified*. Milwaukee, 1974.

Middleton, William D., with George M. Smerk and Roberta L. Diehl. *Encyclopedia of North American Railroads*. Bloomington and Indianapolis, IN, 2007.

Mika, Nick, with Helma Mika. *Railways of Canada*. Toronto and Montreal, 1972.

Miner, Craig H. *The St. Louis-San Francisco Transcontinental Railroad*. Lawrence, KS, 1972.

Mohowski, Robert E. *New York, Ontario & Western in the Diesel Age*. Andover, NJ, 1994.

Mott, Edward Harold. *Between the Ocean and the Lakes—The Story of Erie.* New York, 1900.

Murray, Tom. *Canadian National Railway.* St. Paul, MN, 2004.

Myrick, David F. *Life and Times of the Central Pacific Railroad.* 1969.

———. *Western Pacific—The Last Transcontinental Railroad.* Colorado Rail Annual No. 27. CO, 2006.

Overton, Richard, C. *Burlington Route.* New York, 1965.

———. *Burlington West.* Cambridge, MA, 1941.

Potter, Janet Greenstein. *Great American Railroad Stations.* New York, 1996.

Protheroe, Ernest. *The Railways of the World.* London, n.d.

Quiett, Glenn Chesney. *They Built the West.* New York, 1934.

Reed, S. G. *A History of the Texas Railroads.* Houston, TX. 1941.

Riegel, Robert Edgar. *The Story of the Western Railroads.* Lincoln, NE, 1926.

Rosenberger, Homer Tope. *The Philadelphia and Erie Railroad.* Potomac, MD, 1975.

Sabin, Edwin, L. *Building the Pacific Railroad.* Philadelphia, 1919.

Salisbury, Stephen. *No Way to Run a Railroad.* 1982.

Saunders, Richard, Jr. *Main Lines: American Railroads 1970–2002.* DeKalb, IL, 2003.

———. *Merging Lines: American Railroads 1900–1970.* DeKalb, IL, 2001.

———. *The Railroad Mergers and the Coming of Conrail.* Westport, CT, 1978.

Saylor, Roger B. *The Railroads of Pennsylvania.* State College, PA, 1964.

Schafer, Mike, and Brian Solomon. *Pennsylvania Railroad.* Minneapolis, MN, 2009.

Schrenk, Lorenz P., and Robert L. Frey. *Northern Pacific Diesel Era 1945–1970.* San Marino, CA, 1988.

Shaughnessy, Jim. *Delaware & Hudson.* Howell North Books, Berkeley, CA, 1967.

———. *The Rutland Road,* 2nd ed. Syracuse, New York. 1997.

Shearer, Frederick, E. *The Pacific Tourist.* New York, 1970.

Signor, John R. *Beaumont Hill.* San Marino, CA, 1990.

———. *Donner Pass: Southern Pacific's Sierra Crossing.* San Marino, CA, 1985.

———. *Rails in the Shadow of Mt. Shasta.* San Diego, 1982.

———. *Southern Pacific's Coast Line.* Wilton, CA, 1994.

———. *Tehachapi.* San Marino, CA, 1983.

———. *Western Division.* Wilton, CA, 2003.

Smalley, Eugene V. *History of the Northern Pacific Railroad.* New York, 1883.

Smith, Warren L. *Berkshire Days on the Boston & Albany.* New York, 1982.

Solomon, Brian. *The American Diesel Locomotive.* Osceola, WI, 2000.

———. *The American Steam Locomotive.* Osceola, WI, 1998.

———. *Amtrak.* St. Paul, MN, 2004.

———. *Burlington Northern Santa Fe Railway.* St. Paul, MN, 2005.

———. *CSX.* St. Paul, MN, 2005.

———. *Locomotive.* Osceola, WI, 2001.

———. *North American Railroad—the Illustrated Encyclopedia.* Minneapolis, MN, 2012.

———. *Railway Masterpieces: Celebrating the World's Greatest Trains, Stations and Feats of Engineering.* Iola, WI, 2002.

———. *Railroads of California.* Minneapolis, MN, 2009.

———. *Railroads of Pennsylvania.* Minneapolis, MN, 2008.

———. *Railroad Signaling.* St. Paul, MN, 2003.

———. *Southern Pacific Passenger Trains.* St. Paul, MN, 2005.

———. *Super Steam Locomotives.* Osceola, WI, 2000.

———. *Trains of the Old West.* New York, 1998.

Solomon, Brian, and Mike Schafer. *New York Central Railroad.* Osceola, WI, 1999.

Staff, Virgil. *D-Day on the Western Pacific.* Glendale, CA, 1982.

Staufer, Alvin F. *C&O Power.* Carrollton, OH, 1965.

———. *Pennsy Power III.* Medina, OH, 1993.

———. *Steam Power of the New York Central System,* vol. 1. Medina, OH, 1961.

Staufer, Alvin F., and Edward L. May. *New York Central's Later Power.* Medina, OH, 1981

Starr, John W. *One Hundred Years of American Railroading.* Millersburg, PA, 1927.

Stevens, Frank W. *The Beginnings of the New York Central Railroad.* New York, 1926.

Stover, John F. *History of the New York Central Railroad.* New York, 1975.

———. *The Life and Decline of the American Railroad.* New York, 1970.

———. *The Routledge Historical Atlas of the American Railroads.* New York, 1999.

Swengel, Frank M. *The American Steam Locomotive: Vol. 1, Evolution.* Davenport, IA, 1967.

Taber, Thomas Townsend, III. *The Delaware, Lackawanna & Western Railroad, Part One.* Williamsport, PA,. 1980.

Talbot, F. A. *Railway Wonders of the World,* vol. 1 and 2. London, 1914.

Thompson, Gregory Lee. *The Passenger Train in the Motor Age.* Columbus, OH, 1993.

Thompson, Slason. *The Railway Library—1912.* Chicago, 1913.

———. *Short History of American Railways.* Chicago, 1925.

Trewman, H. F. *Electrification of Railways.* London, 1920.

Turner, Gregg M., and Melancthon W. Jacobus. *Connecticut Railroads.* Hartford, CT, 1989.

Vance, James E., Jr. *The North American Railroad.* Baltimore, 1995.

Walker, Mike. *Appalachia and Piedmont.* Feaversham, Kent, UK, 1997.

———. *California and Nevada.* Feaversham, Kent, UK, 1996.

———. *Great Lakes East.* Feaversham, Kent, UK, 1997.

———. *Great Lakes West.* Feaversham, Kent, UK, 1996.

———. *Mountain Plains.* Feaversham, Kent, UK, 2000.

———. *New England & Maritime Canada.* Feaversham, Kent, UK, 1999.

———. *Pacific Northwest.* Feaversham, Kent, UK, 1997.

———. *Southeast.* Feaversham, Kent, UK, 1999.

———. *Southern States.* Feaversham, Kent, UK, 2001.

———. *Steam Powered Video's Comprehensive Railroad Atlas of North America—North East U.S.A.* Feaversham, Kent, UK, 1993.

———. *Texas.* Feaversham, Kent, UK, 2001.

Waters, L. L. *Steel Trails to Santa Fe.* Lawrence, KS, 1950.

Weller, John, L. *The New Haven Railroad—Its Rise and Fall.* New York, 1969.

Westing, Frederic. *Penn Station: Its Tunnels and Side Rodders.* Seattle, 1977.

Westing, Frederic, and Alvin F. Staufer. *Erie Power.* Medina, OH, 1970.

White, John H., Jr., *The American Railroad Passenger Car,* vols. 1 and 2. Baltimore, 1978.

————. *A History of the American Locomotive—Its Development: 1830–1880.* Baltimore,. 1968.

————. *Early American Locomotives.* Toronto, 1979.

Williams, Harold A. *The Western Maryland Railway Story.* Baltimore, MD, 1952.

Wilner, Frank N. *The Amtrak Story.* Omaha, NE, 1994.

Wilson, Neill C., and Frank J. Taylor. *Southern Pacific: The Roaring Story of a Fighting Railroad.* New York, 1952.

Wilson, O. Meredith. *The Denver and Rio Grande Project, 1870–1901.* Salt Lake City, 1982.

Winchester, Clarence. *Railway Wonders of the World,* vol. 1 and 2. London, 1935.

Wright, Richard K. *Southern Pacific Daylight.* Thousand Oaks, CA, 1970.

PERIODICALS

American Railroad Journal and Mechanics' Magazine [no longer published].

Baldwin Locomotives [no longer published]. Philadelphia, PA.

CTC Board. Ferndale. Washington

Jane's World Railways. London.

Moody's Analyses of Investments, Part I—Steam Railroads. New York.

Pacific RailNews [no longer published]. Waukesha, WI.

Railroad History [formerly *Railway and Locomotive Historical Society Bulletin*]. Boston, MA.

Official Guide to the Railways. New York

Railway and Locomotive Engineering [no longer published]. New York.

Railway Age. Chicago and New York.

Railway Gazette, 1870–1908 [no longer published]. New York.

The Railway Gazette. London.

TRAINS Magazine. Waukesha, WI.

Vintage Rails [no longer published]. Waukesha, WI.

Washington Post. Washington, D.C.

BROCHURES, TIMETABLES, RULE BOOKS AND REPORTS

Amtrak. Public timetables 1971–2011.

Boston & Albany Railroad. *Time-Table No. 174.* 1955.

Boston & Albany Railroad. *Facts about the Boston & Albany R.R.* 1933.

Burlington Northern Santa Fe Corporation. *Annual Reports 1996–2004.*

Burlington Northern Santa Fe Railway. Grade profiles. n.d.

Burlington Northern Santa Fe Railway. *System Map.* 2003.

Canadian National. *2007 Annual Report.*

Chicago, Milwaukee, St. Paul & Pacific. Public timetables 1943–1966.

Chicago Operating Rules Association. *Operating Guide,* 1994.

Conrail. *Pittsburgh Division, System Timetable No. 5.* 1997.

CSX Transportation. *Baltimore Division, Timetable No. 2.* 1987.

CSX Transportation. *System Map.* 1999.

Delaware, Lackawanna & Western. *A Manual of the Delaware, Lackawanna & Western.* 1928.

Erie Railroad. *Erie Railroad its Beginnings and Today.* 1951.

Interstate Commerce Commission. *Fourth Annual Report on the Statistics of Railways of the United States for the year ended June 30, 1891.* Washington, D.C., 1892.

General Code of Operating Rules, Fourth Edition. 2000.

Metro-North Railroad. *Rules of the Operating Department.* 1999.

Metro-North Railroad. *Timetable No. 1.* 2001.

New York Central System. *Rules for the Government of the Operating Department.* 1937.

New York Central System. Public timetables 1943–1968.

NORAC. *Operating Rules,* 7th ed. 2000

Pennsylvania Railroad. Public timetables 1942–1968.

Richmond Fredericksburg and Potomac Railroad Company. *Timetable No. 31.* 1962.

Santa Fe. Public timetables 1943–1964.

Sen. Doc. 119, 73d Congress, 2d Session. *Report of Federal Coordinator of Transportation on Regulation of Railroads.* January 20, 1934.

Southern Pacific Company. *Pacific System Time Table No. 17, Coast Division.* 1896.

Southern Pacific Company. Public timetables 1930–1958

Southern Pacific. *Your Daylight Trip.* 1939.

INTERNET SOURCES

www.aar.org
www.ble.org
www.bnsf.com
www.cn.ca
www.cpr.ca
www.csx.com
www.fecrwy.com
www.fra.dot.gov
www.guilfordrail.com
www.gwrr.com
www.kcsouthern.com
www.modot.org
www.montanarail.com
www.nscorp.com
www.railamerica.com
www.uprr.com
www.vermontrailway.com
www.wnyprr.com
www.wsorrailroad.com

INDEX